Bipartisan Battlefields

The Definitive Guide to U.S Political Issues

by
Thomas T. Taylor

Dear Esteemed Reader,

Thank you immensely for choosing this book to join your collection. We imagine that you've already embarked on an exploration of ideas within these pages, and we couldn't be happier about it!

Now, if you find yourself chuckling, pondering, or even debating with the words in front of you, we'd absolutely love to hear about it. If you can spare a few moments to pen down your thoughts in a review, we would be as delighted as a dictionary on a spelling bee!

An Amazon review would be excellent - but hey, we're far from picky. Whether it's a scribble on the back of a grocery list, a tweet, or even a message in a bottle (though that might take a while to reach us), your feedback is gold.

Writing a review might not be as fun as a spontaneous dance-off, but we promise it'll bring grins to our faces, warmth to our hearts, and incredibly valuable insights to future readers.

With Gratitude,

Bo Bennett, PhD
Publisher
Archieboy Holdings, LLC.

Table of Contents

Introduction

Information is a powerful tool. With it, we are more than just citizens; we are informed voters, active participants in the democratic process. But in a political landscape that often seems like a battlefield, full of passionate debates, stark disagreements, and contradictory voices, how do we make sense of it all? This book is designed to help you examine the nuances of the American political system, elucidating both Republican and Democratic perspectives on a whirlwind of critical issues from healthcare reform to climate change policy. But it doesn't stop at simply laying out the facts. We'll also delve into the vital role of unbiased information in making informed political decisions, the impact of extreme views, and ways to foster bipartisan collaboration. So let's dive in, for the true power of an informed voter begins with understanding.

Understanding the Bipartisan Battlefield

In the arena of American politics, there's a fierce battlefield that's rarely seen by casual viewers. It's a landscape filled with nuances and intricacies, with every word, decision, and policy carrying weight that could tilt the scales one way or the other. This is the bipartisan battlefield, where Republicans and Democrats lock horns on key issues, pressing their viewpoints while trying to secure support for their perspectives.

When seen from the outside, this battlefield may seem like a hostile and divisive terrain. But once you delve deeper, it's evident how this landscape shapes, molds and drives the nation's political discourse.

Each side is armed with its core ideals and values, all stemming from their defined philosophies and comprehensive principles. Intersecting at the point of these principles are the policies and initiatives that make the workings of a nation possible.

Here, you can see the dynamics of the two-party system that the United States has followed since its inception. While it sometimes seems like an almighty clash, it's necessary for creating a balanced, equitable, and progressive society. The essence of this conflict can be found in the tug-of-war between maintaining cherished traditions and advancing towards a future that aligns with evolving understandings.

Being a Republican or a Democrat is about much more than adhering to party lines or picking a side on an issue. It's about fundamentally different worldviews clashing and attempting to find a middle ground. Sometimes, that middle ground is elusive, and that's when the battlefield becomes more intense.

On one end of the spectrum, Republicans believe in the power of the free market, individual liberty, and limited government. They champion personal responsibility, military strength, and traditional values. At the other end, Democrats advocate for social equality, civil rights, and welfare programs, investing faith in the government's role in ensuring fairness and providing support for citizens.

These varying ideals often create friction, but this friction is critical to the democratic process. This challenge of differing ideologies leads to checks and balances that help maintain a robust political system. But navigating this battlefield, understanding its complications, calls for an effort from all of us. An effort to appreciate and respect the value of differing viewpoints, along with recognizing that progress isn't a one-way street.

Enter the role of the voter. The most important player in this polarized arena. As voters, it's our responsibility to not only cast our votes but to also understand the battlefield in which our chosen candidates operate. Only through a comprehensive comprehension, we can hope to play an educated part in this process, a role that shapes our society's direction.

Let's also remember that this battlefield doesn't exist solely during election seasons. It exists in Congress, in local governments, in our communities, and sometimes even at our dinner tables. It's a constant undercurrent, shaping our beliefs and decisions, and impact lives on both a grand and individual scale.

A necessary step to understanding this battlefield lies in acknowledging its vastness. America is a diverse nation, with each state, city, and community having unique issues and needs. While certain key topics often dominate the discourse, they merely scratch the surface of the complex tapestry that forms the bipartisan battlefield.

Aside from these broad themes, there's a multitude of policies and regulations where partisan dynamics are at play. Take for instance healthcare reform, climate change policies, immigration policy, gun control, political correctness, voting rights, education reform, abortion, inflation management, budgeting, crime prevention, national debt management, and foreign policy, just to name a few. These issues spark debates and disagreements within the bipartisan battlefield as parties strive to shape these initiatives according to their political principles.

That being said, the battlefield isn't just about conflicts, it's also about collaboration. While they may disagree on the ways to get there, both Republicans and Democrats aim to create a prosperous, safe, and just America. Recognizing this common goal allows for sincere dialogue, compromise, and negotiation—the cornerstone of any functioning democracy.

Ultimately, understanding the bipartisan battlefield is about accepting its inherent conflicts while appreciating the opportunities it provides. It's about valuing the presence of different mindsets and enabling them to contribute to the best outcome for the nation.

Each one of us has the power to shape the policies and the people that define our national, state, and local governments. To use this power effectively, it's pertinent we understand the essence of the bipartisan battlefield, the principles that guide it, and the common purpose that unites both sides. For a thriving democracy, a savvy electorate is paramount, and our journey as informed voters begins here.

Chapter 1:
The Role of Unbiased Information in Political Decisions

As we venture into the heart of unbiased information, can't we all agree that it's a crucial element in the realm of political decisions? In the heats of debates and the chaos of campaigns, facts and uncolored data form the bedrock of informed choices. Let's imagine the political landscape as a wild, tumultuous sea. Political parties, candidates, and policies are the vessels that navigate these waters, while citizens are the sailors making constant decisions about their course. Just as sailors need reliable charts and sound meteorological data, voters require fact-based, unbiased information to make enlightening choices. Inevitably, the absence or distortion of such information fosters ignorance that fuels polarization and blind party-targeting, reducing complex political issues to oversimplified binary choices. That's why unbiased information, both in breadth and depth, is vitally important. By dismissing color and personal feelings, can't we provide a better understanding of the critical political issues at hand? This understanding, in turn, encourages informed decision-making, which is instrumental in forming more effective government policies and creating a more participatory democracy. In fact, it's not merely important - it's essential, just as a compass is to a sailor navigating the vast, unpredictable sea.

Against Ignorance: The Importance of Factual Knowledge

Ignorance is a complicated condition and an inescapable part of the human experience. It often stems from a lack of awareness or education, a resolute naivety, or even from deliberate choice. In the scope of politics, ignorance can be dangerous as it results in uninformed decisions. Factual knowledge, therefore, plays an essential role as it fosters an environment for sound decision-making.

Ignorance in politics shouldn't be dismissed as mere naivety. It comes accompanied by a dangerous element: misinformation. Misinformation is not just a lack of information, but it points to incorrect, nonfactual data which skews people's perceptions. Correcting misinformation is often more challenging than delivering new, accurate information. Hence, reinforcing the importance of deploying factual knowledge in political discourse.

Humankind universally depends on shared knowledge to maintain civilizations. This shared knowledge, or public knowledge, constitutes facts that are indisputable. From the laws of physics to actual events in history, these facts form part of our societal structure. In politics, this public knowledge is crucial in ensuring informed discussions and decision-making processes.

Public knowledge in democracy serves as the foundation on which political debates and decisions rest. It provides a shared understanding and a common ground for discussions. Our political arena becomes skewed when this foundation is ignored or undermined for political gains.

Discrediting the facts sets a dangerous precedent and threatens the very fabric of democratic discourse. This is often evident when political leaders and media outlets play fast and loose with facts for short-term political gains, leading to long-term ramifications.

Factual knowledge does not mean everyone will interpret it the same way. It's like two artists looking at a sunset: they might agree on the color of the sky but have vastly different aesthetic evaluations. In politics, this is a healthy way to create multiple viewpoints, which are the essence of political diversity in democracy.

However, the problem occurs when the facts themselves are disputed. If the facts are represented incorrectly or manipulated, it leads to a volatile political climate where there is significant disaccord. The act of dismissing established facts distorts the nature of the political discourse and inhibits productive conversation.

On the other hand, encouraging factual knowledge offers numerous benefits. It fosters responsible citizenship, enabling voters to make informed decisions. Factual knowledge promotes accountability, compelling leaders to be transparent and act ethically. It increases clarity and decreases misunderstanding, helping to prevent manipulation or misinformation.

An emphasis on fact-checking and due diligence becomes vital in such an environment. As voters, we must strive to fact-check any information we're being fed before rallying behind political parties, and platforms we align with.

A potent defense against ignorance is education. Education does not only relay information, it also teaches individuals how to sensibly process and evaluate it. An educated electorate is less likely to play into misinformation or manipulation, thereby making the democratic process more effective.

Beyond formal education, the importance of self-education should not be undermined. Self-education encourages independent research and thought, leading to well-rounded opinions. Some of the most effective tools for self-education include reading diverse sources of news, analyzing data, and continually asking questions. This helps in discerning fact from fiction.

What's critical in this pursuit of knowledge, though, is developing an openness to information that contradicts our beliefs or challenges our convictions. It's natural to gravitate towards information that affirms what we already think, but it's equally important to listen to diverse perspectives. This openness to contrary information is a sign of intellectual maturity and encourages a healthy, robust democratic dialogue.

Even as we strive to dispel ignorance, we must remember that it's a ceaseless expedition. There is always more to learn, more to understand. A healthy democracy requires constant vigilance, fact-checking and an ongoing commitment to education. This perpetuation of learning makes an electorate robust and resilient.

In conclusion, factual knowledge combats ignorance, making it instrumental in any political decision-making process. An electorate privileged with factual knowledge is more likely to make informed decisions that bring about effective change. Unraveling a well-informed and educated society capable of critical thinking isn't a walk in the park. However, it's an investment with dividends that make the effort well worth it across the bipolar battlefield that politics often is.

The Impact of Extreme Views

The force of extremism in politics, while potentially invigorating, often undermines the balanced dialogue needed to forge constructive policies. Due to their inherently oppositional and non-negotiable stances, extreme views tend to generate a deterring effect on unbiased political decision-making. Laying out a fact-sheet or presenting a well-reasoned argument fails to influence when the listener is overwhelmingly aligned with an extreme view. Such entrenched ideologies can disrupt the objectivity required for clear political judgements and can lead to reliance on biased information. While it's valid to suggest that extreme perspectives might occasionally kick-start stagnant policy discussions, it's also essential to keep in mind that they can create a stubborn divide, discouraging collaboration and compromise. Moreover, extreme beliefs, being high in emotive content, often sway voters towards confirmation bias, thereby impoverishing the quality of political decisions. As such, to enhance the effectiveness of unbiased information in political decisions, it's vital to address the impact of extreme views on broad political discourse.

Polarization Fueled by Ignorance can be seen as one of the most threatening of all divisive forces within the political arena. It's a factor born out of a lack of sufficient, unbiased facts coupled with the human tendency to resist changing their beliefs. This powerful combustible mix can render even the most logical and factual arguments powerless, paving way for heated debates and irrational decision making.

Examine for a moment, a society divided over a policy based not on their understanding, but rather out of party loyalties or parental influence. This lack of comprehension often results in individuals gravitating towards one extreme or the other without fully understanding the nuances or consequences of their decision. Being uninformed about nuances makes a person unable or less likely to recognize the problems with extreme positions, leading to a kind of blind partisanship that can easily morph into extremism.

Those who are uninformed or ill-informed tend to ground their perspectives in misconceptions, often attaching emotional importance to them, and will usually not be swayed by factual data or rational argument. Their biases, fueled by ignorance, perpetuate an 'us against them' narrative. It's not partisanship, but ignorance, a severe lack of understanding or desire to understand, that deep-divides a society. It's when citizens are not able to discern actual facts from propaganda and end up adopting polarized positions based on what 'seems right' according to their preferred media, peer groups, or societal norms.

The impact of this can be profound, leading to a stagnated political environment wherein decisions are not based on sound knowledge or understanding of the issues at hand, but rather by which side of the divide someone belongs to. Moreover, it feeds into the destructive cycle for political polarization, as those who cling to their ignorance or reject counteracting information become even more steadfast in their polarized views. This widens the divide, making it increasingly hard to find common ground or engage in informed, productive conversations about political issues.

Addressing the issue of ignorance fueling polarization needs an active push towards promoting political literacy and critical thinking among the public. Within this arena, the ability to critique the news, discern facts from biases, and uphold an understood and shared democratic values system becomes particularly vital. Educating voters isn't just about policy specifics or historical context but also about fostering the ability to critically appraise information and understand the inherent complexity of political issues. This could gradually break down the barriers built by ignorance, allowing for a more nuanced understanding of the issues at hand, thus helping in mitigating polarization.

Blind Acceptance of Party Positions is an unfortunately common occurrence in the realm of political discourse. It refers to the inclination of voters to support the stance of their chosen political party, often without a deeper understanding or analysis of the issue at hand.

Why do voters fall for this? Party positions serve as a beacon, guiding voters amidst the vast complexities of modern political issues. One reason for this blind acceptance is the sense of identity and community a party provides. This tribal instinct - the human desire to align with a group - can lead to unwavering allegiance toward the party line, even when the position may counter a voter's personal interest or belief. This comfort in identification can be a powerful motivator, especially in times of political polarization and conflict.

Another contributing factor is the influence of media. The modern information era has its share of challenges, particularly the rise of misinformation and the propensity of media outlets to cater to specific political ideologies, creating an echo chamber for viewers. This media bias often amplifies the party's message and can lead to the uncritical acceptance of party positions. The danger here isn't just the acceptance of a political stance without scrutiny, but the often inadvertent internalization of an entire ideological agenda.

Moving beyond blind allegiance is not a call to renounce party affiliation, but rather a plea for critical thinking. To do so, voters must actively engage in obtaining unbiased information and foster open conversations that encourage differing views. A robust democracy thrives not on uniformity, but on the diversity of thought.

Ultimately, the cure for blind acceptance of party positions is a combination of education, engagement, and introspection. This doesn't mean endless debates or confrontational conversations. But it requires a willingness to venture beyond the comfortable horizons of one's party line, to question, investigate, and form an independent judgement. An informed electorate is, after all, the cornerstone of a vibrant democracy.

Chapter 2:
Critical Political Issues

In the complex field of the current political landscape, there are key issues that draw universal attention and, often, heated debate. These contentious topics encompass the spheres of healthcare, climate change, immigration policy, gun control, political correctness, voting rights, the state of our educational system, matters of life and decision, economic issues like inflation and the budget deficit, criminal justice, national debt, and foreign policy. All these are instrumental subjects in shaping legislation, swaying votes, and defining the ideologies central to the different political parties.

Healthcare reform continues to steer political discourse, with the Republican and Democratic parties both prioritizing — but defining — the issue differently. Such variation in values and proposed solutions can also be found across discussion on climate change policy, where political views often align with conflicting scientific interpretations and economic considerations. The solvency of immigration policy, or lack thereof, is also a pressing matter, flanked by differing ideas of border control, path to citizenship, and humanitarian principles. The battle over gun control hangs in the balance of upholding Second Amendment rights and addressing gun violence, whereas debates on political correctness probe the intersection of free speech and the societal demand for increased sensitivity and awareness. Questions of election integrity versus voting rights complicate our democratic practices and their evolving boundaries.

The pendulum of political concern also swings towards education reform, where disagreements often stem from the balance between federal and state control, standardized testing, and the position of charter schools in our system. Polarizing viewpoints surround abortion as well, revolving around considerations of women's rights, religious beliefs, and the definition of life itself. Economic challenges, including inflation issues, debt, and the budget deficit demand attention against the backdrop of an ever-fluctuating global market. Similarly, approaches towards crime and the justice system loom over discussions on mandatory sentencing and prison reform. The long-standing matter of the national debt prompts examination on the wisdom of long-term borrowing and sparking contemplation on our nation's fiscal responsibility. Last but not least, foreign policy—the United States' interaction with other nations—rounds out our brief survey of critical political issues, underscoring the varying outlooks on intervention, diplomacy, and global economic cooperation.

Healthcare Reform

The issue of healthcare reform remains a quintessential topic in political discourse, and it's especially significant when understanding the vast ideological divide between Republicans and Democrats in America. Central to the debate is how best to provide, pay for, and regulate the healthcare necessary for millions of Americans. Both sides understand that healthcare is a cornerstone of civilized society; however, the means to achieve optimal healthcare reform presents a chronic challenge.

One central facet of this polarized debate is whether healthcare should primarily exist as a private or public entity. The private sector approach, predominantly favored by Republicans, leans towards less government interference, promoting competition, and efficiency. Alternatively, Democrats cooperate with elements of the private sector but generally believe that the government has a larger role in assuring access to affordable, quality health care.

The crux of the healthcare reform debate often revolves around issues like affordability, quality of care, and access to services. For many, the profound inequities in healthcare, especially regarding racial and socio-economic disparities, are more than just policy debates. These are urgent, real-world issues that impact their lives every day.

In the spotlight of healthcare reform is the Patient Protection and Affordable Care Act (ACA), commonly known as Obamacare. The ACA was envisioned to improve access to and the quality of healthcare. The goal of the ACA was to reduce the number of uninsured by providing affordable, quality health insurance and to reduce the growth in healthcare spending.

However, the ACA has been a contentious point of political divide with significant disagreement on its effectiveness. Economic considerations, philosophical differences, and divergent views on the role of government have all contributed to a complex, often heated debate around this landmark healthcare legislation.

The discourse on healthcare reform is not just about policy—it's about people. It's about the strain or ease with which families can seek medical help without fear of debilitating debt. It's about enabling all American citizens to have an equal chance at leading healthy, productive lives, irrespective of their income or social standing.

Amid this debate, complexities around the existing healthcare system surface. These include the undertaking of creating a centralized approach in a federal system where states have traditionally managed the health of their citizens. There are also considerations of fear towards change—fear of higher taxes, fear of long waiting times and reduced choice, misconceptions that pervade the discourse around universal healthcare.

Furthermore, industrial forces play a significant role in shaping health policy—pharmaceutical companies, insurance firms, medical technologies, and service providers are powerful stakeholders and are often resistant to changes that could affect their bottom line. Balancing these interests while providing quality, affordable care presents a formidable challenge for policymakers.

Beyond delivering affordable, high-quality healthcare, the discourse on healthcare reform also addresses preventative healthcare. Engaging in preventive strategies such as vaccinations, screenings, and education can lower healthcare costs in the long run by addressing health issues before they escalate into serious and costly medical emergencies.

Additionally, America's aging population presents another significant challenge in the healthcare reform debate. The skyrocketing costs of caring for an increasingly older population, often with complex and chronic health conditions, demands urgent attention and innovative solutions.

The healthcare reform discourse not merely centers on economics and policy but intersects with ethical and moral considerations about what sort of society Americans want to cultivate. It begs questions about the obligations we have to our fellow citizens, the trade-offs we are willing to accept, and the price we are ready to pay to ensure quality healthcare access for all.

Healthy citizens form the foundation of a robust, vibrant society. By marginalized individuals receiving the health services they desperately require, these individuals are capable of leading meaningful lives and making valuable contributions to their communities. The challenge lies in crafting the policy that effectively delivers on this promise.

As voters, we are all stakeholders in this critical issue. The healthcare reform debate is a complex, multi-tiered issue that offers no easy solutions. As such, it necessitates our active, informed participation to ensure that the decisions made genuinely represent our needs—and the needs of every American citizen.

Republican Stance on Healthcare Reform

As we delve into the heart of the Republican stance on healthcare reform, there's an emphasis on a market-based system where competition, consumer choice, and the principles of supply and demand govern the industry. These core beliefs resonate strongly with the tenets of fiscal conservatism and limited government interference, the hallmark of the Republican philosophy.

Primarily, Republicans view government intrusion into healthcare as a detrimental factor. They argue that it stifles innovation and competition, instead, they suggest the government's role should be not that of controlling but of facilitating a competitive health market. Republicans espouse the idea of people being able to shop for their health insurance as they would for any other good or service, which they believe would naturally lead to a decrease in healthcare costs and improved quality of services.

Their perspective on health insurance leans more towards individual responsibility and less on social safety nets. Republicans have championed health savings accounts as crucial elements for individuals to cover medical expenses and often propose tax credits as an avenue of making insurance accessible. The idea here is to incentivize healthcare providers to compete for business, theoretically leading to an increase in efficiency and quality.

Medicaid, a significant part of the national debate, has had Republicans express concerns about its rapid expansion and costs. They have generally proposed block-grant funding to states, providing them more discretion on how to utilize those funds, believing state governments better understand the needs and unique situations of their residents. This is consistent with their doctrine of decentralized government where decision-making power should be close to those affected by the policies.

It's critical to note that Republicans do acknowledge the need to protect individuals with pre-existing conditions, a point of contention in the healthcare debate. Their approach, however, differs significantly. The emphasis is on affordable access rather than guaranteed coverage.

Pharmaceutical pricing has been an area of bipartisan focus and agreement. Republicans, in this case, deviate somewhat from the laissez-faire approach and support governmental intervention in regulating drug prices intending to make essential medicines affordable and accessible to the general population.

Summarily, the Republican stance on healthcare reform encapsulates their broader ideological perspective on matters of national concern: The solution to societal problems lies not in government-led initiatives, but rather in the dynamism and creativity of a free market, the sensibilities of state governments, and the ability of the individual to make decisions that best align with their unique circumstances.

Democratic Stance on Healthcare Reform Now, let's divert our attention to the Democratic approach to healthcare. Constituting a significant slice of the party's agenda, Democrats advocate for expanding access to quality healthcare, emphasizing the principle that healthcare is a right, not a privilege. They prioritize making healthcare more accessible and affordable and ensuring that pre-existing conditions do not impede access to healthcare coverage.

Aligning with this ideological outlook, Democrats are also the proponents of the Affordable Care Act, indelibly termed as "Obamacare", a statute that extended health insurance to millions of uninsured Americans. They have expressed resistance against attempts to repeal or undermine the law, underpinning the significance of securing healthcare access for everyone, irrespective of their income level.

In essence, Democrats tend to favor an active role for government in health care, with the ultimate aim of providing universal health care coverage. Their measures to achieve this end typically involve expanding publicly funded health care programs, like MediCare and MediCaid, along with advocating for the protection of consumer rights in the healthcare sector.

Another key focus area within the Democrats' health care agenda is mental health. They aim to break the stigma attached to mental health by ensuring equal esteem for mental and physical health, bridging the service gap through health care reform, and facilitating wider access to mental health services.

On prescription drug pricing, a matter of recurring public concern, Democrats favor action requiring drug manufacturers to disclose how they set their prices. They advocate for importing lower-priced drugs from other countries, negotiating MediCare drug prices, and allowing consumers to buy prescription drugs from online pharmacies.

Addressing health disparities and endorsing health equity also remain a core objective of their stand. This includes measures aimed at reducing racial, ethnic, and socioeconomic disparities in health outcomes, particularly those stemming from differences in quality of health care, access to healthcare, and certain social determinants of health.

Finally, Democratic viewpoints on abortion contrast with their Republican counterparts. They generally affirm a woman's right to make decisions regarding her reproductive health, which includes access to safe, legal abortion. They also support family planning services, birth control accessibility and comprehensive sex education in schools.

To sum up in a nutshell, the Democratic stance on healthcare is shaped by a commitment to universal health care coverage, advocacy for affordable health care, addressing health disparities, protection of reproductive rights, and a focus on mental health services. While this broad stance doesn't represent every Democratic voter or lawmaker, it provides a lens through which to understand the party's guiding principles and objectives in healthcare policy.

Climate Change and Environmental Policy

As we delve into the politically charged topic of climate change and environmental policy, it becomes clear that this issue transcends boundaries of state, nation, and party. It's an issue that affects us all, and one that has repeatedly shown up in the political arena with increasing urgency. The effects of climate change, from devastating wildfires to unprecedented storms, render it an undeniable priority.

A principal facet of climate change revolves around its overarching problem – the planet's rising temperatures, brought about by increasing levels of greenhouse gases in the atmosphere. The resultant ripple effects, namely melting polar ice caps, rising sea levels, exacerbated natural disasters, habitat destruction, and weather pattern disruptions, form a somber picture of our planet's potential future.

Undeniably, the face of climate change is more than just a warming planet. Issues like deforestation, ocean acidification, land degradation, and loss of biodiversity contribute to and exacerbate the problem, creating a multifaceted web of interconnected issues with far-reaching consequences.

Environmental policy, in turn, is the mode by which nations seek to combat these daunting challenges. Through regulation, conservation efforts, renewable energy investment and more, policies are shaped to protect our living spaces, both terrestrial and marine, and the various forms of life that they house.

Environmental policy-making is complex, due in part to the diversity of issues and their broad impacts. From emission standards for industries to fuel economy regulations for vehicles, from endangered species protections to water quality controls, these policies have sweeping implications for our economies, societies, and everyday lives.

The development and enforcement of these policies involve a myriad of institutions at different levels. Governments, international organizations, non-profit groups and even private businesses all play crucial roles in shaping the trajectory of these policies and their success, or lack thereof.

The history of environmental policy in the United States has been marked by significant milestones. One such landmark event was the establishment of the Environmental Protection Agency (EPA) in 1970, tasked with protecting human health and the environment through federal research, monitoring, standard-setting and enforcement activities.

A crucial facet of environmental policy revolves around international cooperation. Climate change, being a global phenomenon, necessitates global solutions. Policies, therefore, have to be coordinated at an international level, with multilateral agreements such as the Paris Agreement standing testament to this effort.

Enforcement, too, is a crucial element in successful environmental policy. Regulations and standards are only effective if properly implemented and adequately enforced. Insufficient enforcement or accountability measures can weaken even the most well-conceived policies.

Environmental policy also bears an intimate link with economic policy. The transition to cleaner, more sustainable industries necessitates investments in renewable energy, green infrastructure, and other sustainable practices. All of these have far-reaching implications for the job market, trade balances, and the overall economic health of the nation.

Towards this end, concepts like a 'green economy' or a 'green new deal' have entered the political lexicon, underlining the intersection of environmental and economic policy. These ideas aim to promote economic growth and job creation while simultaneously addressing environmental challenges.

However, there are valid concerns and challenges with this approach. The economic impacts of stringent environmental regulations may disproportionately affect certain industries and communities, leading to job losses and economic downturns in these areas. Striking a balance between environmental sustainability and economic prosperity is also a constant challenge and a crucial aspect of effective policy-making.

Equally important is the role of science and technology in our battle against environmental degradation. From cleaner energy sources to carbon sequestration technology, from bioengineering to nature-based solutions, advancements in this sector are critical tools for tackling climate change and other environmental challenges.

The dialogue on climate change and environmental policy is dynamic and continually evolving, often steeped in scientific uncertainty and economic speculation. The spectrum of viewpoints and interests makes the policy-making process both complicated and vitally crucial. It's a discussion that we all need to understand and participate in, for the survival and prosperity of our planet and future generations depends on it.

Republican Stance on Climate Change and Environmental Policy

Among many constituents and lawmakers within the Republican party, there persists a degree of skepticism regarding the severity and origins of climate change. While this doesn't mean that Republicans as a whole reject the concept, it's essential to realize that there's a broad range of views within the party about the urgency and nature of this issue.

For instance, some Republicans acknowledge the global scientific consensus that human activity significantly contributes to climate change. Yet, they might challenge the effectiveness and fairness of policies proposed to mitigate it. Their common argument revolves around the potential economic impact of these initiatives. Particularly, they express concern about potential job losses in various industries and increased costs for consumers.

A common republican perspective might unfold as follows: while environmental protection is indeed important, it mustn't handicap the economy. In this light, the focus leans toward solutions that do not excessively disrupt industries and jobs but still address environmental concerns. For example, many Republicans advocate for incremental changes to rules and regulations that can gradually lower emissions rather than immediate, drastic actions.

Further, the party has shown growing interest in promoting market-driven solutions and innovation to tackle environmental issues. This encompasses support for nuclear energy, carbon capture technologies, and natural gas as a 'cleaner' alternative among fossil fuels. Recent years have also seen appeals for an "all of the above" energy strategy, emphasizing the utilization of all domestic energy resources, including renewables coupled with traditional fossil fuels.

In terms of policy, Republicans often scrutinize international agreements on climate change, like the Paris Agreement. Seen as potentially disadvantageous for the U.S., republicans argue that these agreements place an unfair burden on America's shoulders, possibly jeopardizing national interests while other significant polluters do not face the same level of scrutiny or responsibility.

Despite some ongoing skepticism or differing perspectives within the party about the nature of climate change, there's a clear shift happening. The voices within the Republican party advocating for active policies on climate change and environmental issues grow louder every year. Younger Republicans, in particular, are increasingly concerned about climate change and call for action from their leaders.

Nevertheless, the Republican stance on climate change and environmental policy remains a complex, multifaceted issue. As with any policy area, views differ across individuals and factions within the party. However, all agree that the conversation and steps forward should involve respect for both economic stability and environmental sustainability.

Democratic Stance on Climate Change and Environmental Policy moves swiftly to embrace the idea that the environment isn't just a collection of pretty sceneries—it's a substantial contributor to our public health, economic growth, and national security. The Democrats advocate for urgent action to fight climate change, viewing it as one of the most significant existential threats facing our planet.

To highlight this, Democrats champion the Paris Agreement, emphasizing global cooperation in the fight against climate change. Apart from advocating for international cooperation, they also emphasize the need for reinvigorating America's commitment to clean energy development and reducing its dependence on fossil fuels, thus creating countless new jobs in the process.

The Democrats' approach to climate change isn't solely a matter of reducing greenhouse gas emissions—it also encompasses an effort to construct a green economy. Advocates within the party posit that, with strategic planning and investment, the transition to a sustainable economy can catalyze job growth, and catapult the U.S. to a leading position in the global clean energy race, pushing the country into a future powered by a clean, sustainable energy system.

Furthermore, Democrats assert that climate policy must also address justice-related concerns. The party recognizes that low-income communities and communities of color often face the harshest impacts of environmental pollution and climate change. As such, Democrats place a strong emphasis on environmental justice and are committed to addressing these disproportionate impacts by prioritizing resources and support for communities most in need.

In essence, Democrats view climate change and environmental sustainability not as mere political debates, but as moral responsibilities. This demonstrates an intentional and robust stance that binds together economic growth, environmental protection, and social justice with the thread of sustainability.

This isn't to say that all Democrats align perfectly in their views or that there aren't differing opinions within the party. However, what does unite them is the understanding, acceptance, and urgent call to action regarding climate change. Equipped with these guiding principles, Democratic policy writes a compelling narrative—one that integrates the environment into every aspect of American life.

Immigration Policy

One of the most heated topics in the political landscape on a global scale is the matter of immigration policy. Immigration, at its core, involves the movement of people from their homelands into a new country. Whether it's for better opportunities, to flee from danger, or to reunite with family, the motivations behind immigration are diverse and personal.

In many ways, immigration policy is about defining national identity. It encompasses the rules and principles which determine who is allowed entrance into the country, length of stay, citizenship eligibility, and other critical elements. It is these guidelines that shape the cultural, economic, and societal aspects of a nation. Sure enough, discussions and debates about immigration policy quickly become complex and emotionally-charged.

Immigration policy isn't simply about borders; it's an interconnected web of humanitarian, economic, and national security concerns. One major consideration is the treatment of refugees and asylum seekers. These are individuals fleeing persecution, violence, or disaster, presenting both moral and international legal obligations for receiving nations. Assessments on the capacity to provide assistance, as well as the impact on the national economy and social fabric, come into play.

An equally important component is the integration of immigrants into their new society once they have arrived. From access to language learning, to availability of jobs, and acceptance within local communities, successful integration is a multi-faceted challenge. Moreover, it is a long-term commitment with profound implications for the social cohesiveness of a nation.

We also have to discuss the economic implications of immigration policies. On one hand, immigrants contribute to the workforce, pay taxes, start businesses, and bolster economic growth in many sectors. On the other hand, there can be economic challenges tied to immigration, such as potential strain on public services or competition for jobs.

Immigration policy also intersects with national security concerns. Ensuring that the border is secure and that those who pose threats are not admitted is a concern for any nation. However, striking the right balance between security concerns and the compassionate treatment of immigrants is a delicate task.

The legality of immigration is another vast minefield. This encompasses the difference between legal and illegal immigration, the processes for each, and the approaches to dealing with individuals in each category. Often, these topics can blend into areas such as law enforcement, the justice system, and human rights.

What makes the discussion on immigration policy even more intricate are the international relations dimensions. Immigration policies can affect relations with other countries, particularly those that are sources of large numbers of immigrants. Furthermore, these policies can have repercussions on a country's diplomatic standing and international reputation.

Moving from the global context, if we zoom into the American immigration policy, the scenario gets even more complex. Historically, America is a nation built on immigration. From the early settlers to modern day newcomers, immigration has been integral to the nation's evolution. It's no surprise that the subject is highly emotive, often invoking discussions about the American Dream and the spirit of the nation.

However, despite this historical tie, there are clear challenges with the American immigration system that have been debated fiercely in recent years. There are calls for comprehensive immigration reform across the board, covering a wide range of issues such as visa allocations, the situation for undocumented immigrants, border control, and refugee and asylum procedures.

Additionally, the American immigration policy also features DACA (Deferred Action for Childhood Arrivals), a policy that deals with the treatment and legal status of people who were brought to the United States as children but don't have legal immigration status. This topic stands as a hot button issue and represents a significant aspect of the immigration policy debate.

So, here we stand, at the threshold of this tricky but crucial issue that indirectly impacts every citizen's life. What we'll discuss next are the different stances of the Republican and Democratic parties on immigration policy. Again, the point here is not to take sides, but to offer insight and empower you, the reader, with factual information to make your own judgment.

Before we delve into that, let's take a brief moment to appreciate the enormity of the issue. Immigration policy is a complex puzzle. Different pieces, such as economics, national security, humanitarianism, and legality, must fit together to form a picture. That image, depending on who you ask, represents a different vision of the United States. With this understanding, we are now more equipped to delve into the specific perspectives of our political parties.

Republican Stance on Immigration Policy is a topic that brings to the surface a mix of emotionally charged discussions and rational policy decisions. Often seen as firm on immigration, the Republican party generally promotes policies that prioritize national security, economic prosperity, and the rule of law.

To distill it down to its core components, the Republican position bestows preference on lawful immigration, highlighting the need for immigrants to enter the country through legal channels. It's a rationale that propagates the idea of fairness, allowing those who have patiently waited for their turn to come forth, and discouraging others from bypassing the procedure through illegal means.

Over the years, Republican lawmakers have actively sought measures to strengthen border security. They view this as a necessary move not merely to prevent unauthorized immigration but also to check the inflow of illicit substances and combat human trafficking. They often emphasize the need for more border patrol agents, advanced technology, and even physical impediments, such as walls in some high-risk sectors.

In addition, the Republican stance leans towards stringent visa enforcement. This translates into ensuring visa overstays, which account for a large percentage of illegal immigration, are curbed effectively. Enhanced monitoring and tracking systems are often floated as viable solutions for this concern.

Furthermore, Republicans frequently advocate for revising the legal immigration process itself. They suggest alterations to the visa lottery system and argue for the merit-based immigration system. This method prioritizes entrants based on skills and economic contributions rather than family ties. It's a controversial proposition, which critics argue might undermine the long-standing tradition of family-based immigration, but proponents believe it serves national interests more effectively in the modern-world scenario.

A distinguishing characteristic of the Republican stance on immigration is their opposition to policies that they believe incentivize illegal immigration. This includes measures such as 'sanctuary city' policies and certain forms of public assistance for undocumented immigrants. Republicans commonly assert that implementing such policies could undermine the rule of law and potentially encourage more illegal immigration.

In the end, it's evident that the Republican stance on immigration is as complex and nuanced as the issue itself. It incorporates perspectives of security, economy, and legality in a convoluted blend of policy proposals and ideological viewpoints. As voters, it's necessary to understand these stances and their implications to make informed decisions and contribute to a constructive dialogue on this crucial issue.

Democratic Stance on Immigration Policy is centered around the idea of America acting as a diverse and welcoming nation. Democrats generally believe in easing immigration processes and providing a pathway to citizenship for undocumented immigrants, especially for those whom America is home, such as "DREAMers"—those brought to the U.S. as children under the Deferred Action for Childhood Arrivals program (DACA).

Drawing a broad outline, the Democratic party often advocates for revamping the present immigration system. They argue the current system, being outdated and ineffective in addressing the complex nature of modern immigration, necessitates several reforms for it to traverse the twenty-first century effectively. Notably, family reunification and keeping families together, irrespective of their immigration status, are among their top priorities. They are staunch critics of policies that involve separating families at the border or deporting law-abiding undocumented immigrants.

Democrats also zealously endorse DACA, which lets individuals brought up since childhood in the U.S. without documentation get a deferment from being deported and be eligible for a work permit. Gradual amnesty and a feasible pathway to citizenship for these immigrants are widely supported, emphasizing those who contribute productively to society and show respect for the rule of law.

The party has consistently advocated for practical border controls, such as utilizing technology, to maintain national security. Nonetheless, Democrats are usually against heavy-handed or expensive ways to fortify the border such as a border-wall, labeling such measures as wasteful expenditure that doesn't efficiently solve the long-standing problem.

Under the realm of refugee policy, Democrats' stance is rooted in the United States' history as a beacon of hope for those fleeing persecution. They tend to be more accepting, and it's not uncommon to see Democratic policymakers calling for increased refugee admissions.

Adding to this, Democrats generally support adjustments to the visa system, striving for an increase in the types and numbers of visas available for workers, students, and special cases. Their goals are calculated to attract highly skilled immigrants and to protect American workers from displacement.

Finally, Democrats also favor the expansion and protection of workers' rights, irrespective of their immigration status. They believe more protections should be in place to combat exploitation and abuse in the workplace, especially in the context of guest worker programs.

While this overview provides a generalized perception of Democratic values regarding Immigration Policy, it should be noted that variations exist within the party. Some Democrats might adhere to stricter immigration control policies, while others could lean more toward liberal stances. The house of Democrats is varied, and immigration, like all policy areas, is subject to regional and personal perspectives within the wider party platform.

Gun Control / Gun Violence

The subject of gun control and gun violence is a hotbed of emotion, deeply ingrained beliefs, and stark realities. As we consider this issue, we must grapple with the twin competing concepts of personal freedom and societal safety. Does a citizen's right to own various types of firearms outweigh the potential threat to the community's overall safety? The tension between these two concerns weaves its way through the interpretation of the Second Amendment, individual rights, legislative strategies, and nationwide violence statistics.

Historically, the Second Amendment has been at the heart of American legal discourse. Its language, "A well regulated Militia, being necessary to the security of a free State, the right of the people to keep and bear Arms, shall not be infringed," has been interpreted various ways over the centuries. Some see it as a validation of an individual's right to own guns for either self-defense or recreational use. Others suggest that it, in fact, refers to a conditional collective right tied to service in a militia.

The significance of a literal versus interpretive reading of this amendment plays out on the stage of federal and state courts. Here, landmark cases like District of Columbia v. Heller and McDonald v. City of Chicago have substantiated an individual's right to keep and bear arms for self-defense within their homes.

However, alongside this discussion around gun ownership, there sits the issue of gun violence in America. A 2017 study in the American Journal of Medicine found that Americans are 25 times more likely to die from gun violence than people in other high-income countries. It's a startling statistic that underscores the severity of this issue.

Moreover, the multiple incidences of mass shooting tragedies have thrust gun violence into the national spotlight. With the heart-wrenching stories of lives lost and communities shattered, the conversation around gun control becomes understandably urgency-fueled and emotionally charged.

Defining 'gun control' itself is an intricate task. At its most basic, 'gun control' entails any law, policy, practice, or proposal designed to restrict or limit the production, sale, transfer, possession, modification, or usage of firearms. But what those restrictions or limitations look like can vary significantly.

It might involve outright bans on certain types of firearms, such as fully automatic weapons or high-capacity magazines. Gun control could also include measures like comprehensive background checks or waiting periods for gun purchases. A 'red-flag' law is another example, where loved ones or law enforcement can petition to temporarily remove firearms from individuals deemed a risk to themselves or others.

The goals of these regulations center predominantly on minimizing gun violence. They focus on keeping firearms out of the hands of those deemed more likely to misuse them - such as convicted felons, individuals with restraining orders, or those with certain mental illnesses.

But these laws are met with counter-arguments. Detractors often question their effectiveness, arguing that those determined to commit crimes will find firearms regardless of laws. They also point out that many mass shootings occur with legally obtained weapons, suggesting these laws might not be as effective as hoped.

Further complications arise when tackling the issue of illegal firearms trafficked on the 'black market.' There is an ongoing debate regarding how best to handle this vast and murky arena of gun procurement that exists outside the scope of regular gun control legislation.

Moreover, the matter of enforcement comes into play. While laws on paper may sound effective, their execution and enforcement can vary significantly. Factors like resource constraints, loopholes in laws, and varying state gun laws can all complicate implementation.

In sum, addressing gun control and gun violence involves walking a thin line between ensuring the safety of the public and preserving the rights of individuals. It requires a closer look at our laws, the sociological factors that contribute to violence, and the effectiveness of potential preventative measures. As we study these issues, it's essential to remember the goal is not to 'win the debate', but to cultivate a safer society for all.

Republican Stance on Gun Control / Gun Violence is significantly influenced by their belief in individual rights and limited government. The party has frequently advocated for the rights of lawful gun owners and the interpretation of the Second Amendment as an individual right to keep and bear arms. Some Republicans argue that rather than more gun control laws, there's a need for better enforcement of existing laws and action against illegal gun markets.

Many Republicans view gun ownership as crucial for self-defense and crime prevention. Their argument suggests that criminals, by definition, do not follow laws and that additional restrictions only burden law-abiding gun owners. Following this perspective, some propose solutions such as armed guards at schools and easing restrictions on carrying concealed weapons as measures to deter potential criminals and reduce gun violence.

The party also supports enhanced mental health programs and acknowledges the role mental illnesses can sometimes play in mass shootings. However, a comprehensive solution that balances civil liberties with gun ownership still seems out of reach. Most Republicans aren't in favor of blanket proposals that could inadvertently limit access to mental health services or stigmatize mental illness.

Within the Republican ranks, of course, there are varying opinions. Some party members support limited forms of gun control, like background checks, red flag laws, and preventing individuals on terrorist watch-lists from purchasing guns. Yet, these voices aren't always in the party's mainstream, especially when the strong influence of gun rights advocacy groups within the GOP is considered.

The challenge remains to find a balance between upholding constitutional rights, maintaining public safety, and managing the reality of gun violence in the United States. How Republicans navigate these painstakingly complex issues will undoubtedly continue to shape the party's position on gun control and gun violence.

Around the issue of gun control, Republican stance offers the scope to delve deeper into a Constitutional interpretation, the desire for limited government intervention in individual lives, societal safety considerations, mental health discussions, and law enforcement's efficacy. The party's perspective offers an insight into a broader understanding of the political landscape and how shared principles can influence specific policy positions.

Democratic Stance on Gun Control / Gun Violence

The Democratic Party has historically advocated for stricter gun control measures, viewing them as necessary to curb gun violence and promote public safety. It's important to understand that this doesn't imply an outright rejection of the Second Amendment. Democrats commonly acknowledge the right to bear arms, but advocate for smart and sensible regulations to reduce gun violence and its tragic impact on society.

The specifics of the Democratic stance on gun control can vary with individual policymakers and regions, however certain proposals come up consistently. Common proposals include the enactment of universal background checks for all gun sales and transfers, including those carried out privately or at gun shows.

Another essential element of the Democratic position is the ban on assault weapons and high-capacity magazines. These types of weaponry, Democrats argue, have no place in the hands of civilians, being specifically designed to maximize casualties in warzones. The consensus is that the availability of these guns contributes to the severity and deadliness of mass shootings.

Other points of focus include raising the legal gun purchasing age to 21 and implementing "red flag" laws. Red flag laws enable family members or law enforcement officers to petition a court to temporarily remove firearms from someone deemed a risk to themselves or others. Such proposals, Democrats argue, could prevent tragedies, including suicides and incidents of domestic violence.

It's worth noting that resistance to these reforms is often depicted as a partisan issue, with Democrats supporting gun control while Republicans oppose it. However, many gun control measures, like universal background checks, enjoy broad public support across demographics and political leanings. As in many other areas, the party's approach to this issue has evolved over time, driven both by rising public concern over mass shootings as well as advocacy from grassroots movements for gun safety.

Paradoxically, data shows that states with stricter gun laws often have fewer gun-related deaths, yet concrete cause-and-effect relationships remain challenging to establish. This is primarily because gun violence is a multifaceted issue tied to mental health, education, domestic violence, poverty, and various other social factors. Subsequently, the Democratic perspective generally supports addressing gun violence through a holistic approach, considering all the related factors.

In conclusion, the Democratic party's stance on gun control centers on advocating for stricter regulations, not the abolition of gun ownership. It recognizes that rights must be balanced with responsibilities, and liberties need not come at the expense of public safety.

Political Correctness / "Wokism"

Following the in-depth discussions ranging from healthcare reform to gun control, we pivot attention towards a somewhat intangible, yet incredibly potent and divisive element shaping current political landscapes: political correctness, or as it has been popularly dubbed, "wokism." It's a phenomenon that echoes through media rooms, school boards, corporate offices, and everyday interactions, influencing how individuals express themselves and interpret the words and actions of others.

At its core, political correctness is the avoidance of language or actions deemed likely to offend or marginalize individuals, particularly those in socially disadvantaged or marginalized groups. It's all about promoting respect, consideration, and fairness in our language choices and actions.

"Wokism," a term birthed from the contemporary "woke" culture, is often used interchangeably with political correctness. The label "woke" was initially intended to describe awareness of social injustices and racial inequalities, but its definition has evolved, encapsulating a broader perception of hyper vigilance towards political correctness and intersectionality.

While seemingly straightforward, these concepts bring to the forefront a torrent of dilemmas and contentious debates, largely concerning freedom of speech, institutional bias, and the ethical boundaries of cultural sensitivity. Striking the balance between ensuring equal respect for all without suppressing free expression is a tightrope walk of societal challenges.

The principle of political correctness aims to tackle preconceived biases and marginalizations entrenched in society. It entails swapping potentially offensive terminologies with more inclusive language, a concept widely prevalent in addressing racial, gender, and disability issues, among others. This approach implicitly acknowledges that the words we use can and do impact others, often in ways we might not initially perceive.

"Wokism," on the other hand, expands this sphere of influence. It's often characterized by a deliberate move towards proactive actions spanning beyond language—championing anti-racism, advocating for LGBTQ+ rights, demanding gender equality, to name but a few. Its manifestation ranges from removing statues of historical figures associated with slavery to integrating gender-neutral bathrooms in public spaces. Wokism is about taking conscious steps to rectify past societal wrongs and establishing a socially equal foundation.

To some, these attempts at cultivating respect and sensitivity spell progress, symbolizing society's evolution towards inclusivity. They view political correctness and wokism as means of promoting societal self-awareness, curbing prejudice, and navigating toward a world where everyone's experiences and identities are valued and respected. These people see it as progress towards a more compassionate and understanding society.

Detractors, however, view these concepts with suspicion or outright contempt. Critics argue that "political correctness" and "wokism" champion censorship and inhibit freedom of speech. They claim these ideologies muffle honest discussions, create a climate of self-censorship, and lead to cancel culture—an environment where public figures and organizations face severe backlash, boycotts, or worse for perceived offenses.

There is also discourse surrounding the risk of virtue signaling, a critique often aimed at wokism. Virtue signaling is the act of expressing views or taking actions solely or chiefly to gain approval within a group, rather than out of genuine concern for the issues at hand. Critics assert that this undermines the true intention of advocacy and dilutes the seriousness of the issues that are being addressed.

Then there's the issue of performative wokeness—an aspect of wokism that props up a socially conscious facade without backing it up with substantial action or policy change. For instance, companies vocally supporting diversity but failing to represent that in their own leadership. Detractors view this as hypocritical spectacle rather than genuine intent to push for societal change.

Implications of this debate extend into education, entertainment, business, and of course, politics. It influences workplace interactions, the creation of films/music/literature, the crafting of business strategies, and how we navigate political discourse. Are institutions too concerned with ticking politically correct boxes rather than fostering authentic inclusivity, or is the push back against political correctness an excuse to protect ingrained prejudices? High stakes questions are rampant, with answers continuing to shape societal norms and values.

In essence, the conversation surrounding political correctness and wokism is an ongoing evolving dialogue about respect, inclusivity, cultural sensitivity, and individual rights in an increasingly diverse society. It's a complex mosaic of stances on language, expression, justice, and equality—a stimulating ideological arena that continues to evolve with society.

As the subsequent segments detail the Republican and Democratic stances on political correctness and wokism, it's important to remember that these are multifaceted concepts with profound implications—far from monolithic doctrines held consistently by all members of either party. It's a testament to the dynamic, intricate weave of our diverse societal tapestry.

Republican Stance on Political Correctness / "Wokism" fluidly transitions from our preceding discussions. To ensure voters are well-educated on this contentious subject, it's essential to analyze Republican viewpoints on political correctness and "wokism".

The Republican party, traditionally, has displayed reticence towards the movement of political correctness. This resistance is often predicated on the assertion that it infringes upon freedom of speech and suppresses diversity of thought. Many Republicans argue that policing language and insisting on certain terminology curbs free discourse, thus obstructing the democratic fabric.

Moreover, many within the party feel that political correctness is employed as a tool for "silencing" or "canceling" voices that dissent from the popular narrative. This apprehension was notably evident in the speeches and various public communications from former President Donald Trump, whose taunts of political correctness struck a chord with a segment of the American populace feeling unheard or misunderstood.

The concept of "wokism", a term which is essentially a critique of a perceived overemphasis on social justice issues, is another facet Republicans often critique. The term "woke", a derivative from African American Vernacular English, previously denoted awareness of social or political injustices, particularly those impacting marginalized groups. However, its recent, more pervasive use has imbued it with a negative connotation amongst conservatives, who interpret the term as shorthand for liberal extremism or virtue signaling.

Many Republicans worry that "wokism" places too high a priority on identity politics, potentially creating societal division rather than unification. They argue that while advocating for the rights and inclusivity of various groups is important, an overemphasis may lead to social fragmentation.

It is essential to note these viewpoints do not ubiquitously represent all Republicans, as party alignment does not guarantee uniformity in opinion. However, the basic tenant of skepticism towards political correctness and "wokism" seems to be a common theme within the party's rhetoric.

Furthermore, while some critics argue that the Republican resistance to political correctness and "wokism" may impede societal progress, others suggest it offers a counterbalance to potential excesses of the left, ensuring robust debate and freedom of expression. Like all complex issues, the multi-faceted layers of political correctness and "wokism" are not easily untangled, underscoring the importance of open-minded conversation.

Ultimately, understanding the Republican viewpoint on this issue is crucial for creating an informed voting decision. For democracy's sake, communication and negotiation across party lines are ideas worth embracing.

Democratic Stance on Political Correctness / "Wokism"

We now turn to the issue of Political Correctness or "Wokism," as it's sometimes called nowadays, from the perspective of the Democratic party. Democrats, as a party, have generally been supportive of this progressive cultural shift, asserting a steadfast commitment to diversity, equity, and inclusivity. They champion for language and actions that respect all individuals, considering such attentiveness crucial in striving for social justice and creating a fair society. Democrats view political correctness not as an accommodation or concession, but as a fundamental evolution towards a more inclusive, tolerant worldview. They often argue that reevaluating our language and societal norms is a necessary part of advancing as a society and creating an equitable world.

This commitment can be seen in the Democratic policy platform, which emphasizes civil rights, gender equality, LGBTQ+ rights, and racial justice. These policies often interpret "wokism" as fundamental for building a more inclusive society, one that values the experiences and rights of all citizens equally. However, critiques suggest this stance can, at times, be too accommodating, leading to policies that prioritize sensitivity over more substantial socio-economic issues, or alienating those who feel their own rights may be neglected in the pursuit of new norms.

Nevertheless, the Democratic stance comes from a desire to see society evolve and improve, believing that this can be accomplished by addressing the system-wide biases present in our language and norms. This position is grounded in a firm belief in the inherent worth of every individual and the necessity of ensuring equal rights, respect, and representation for all.

As we continue navigating this political topic, it's essential to remember that not every Democrat or Democrat-leaning individual adheres absolutely to this view. Like any political group, Democrats are diverse with variations in opinion, and as such, what we've discussed here provides a broad generalization of the party's overall stance.

However we view it, "wokism" is a manifestation of a wider conversation about justice, representation, and respect in society. The Democrats' stance on this issue reflects their dedication to civil rights, equity, and social justice. Yet, like any stance, it's vital we consider it with a discerning eye, critically analyzing its benefits and consequences in our drive towards a more enlightened society.

Election Integrity / Voting Rights

Election integrity and voting rights are unquestionably fundamental to any democratic system. They constitute the foundation upon which societies shape their laws and policies, elect leaders, and facilitate progress. At their core, these topics deal with who can vote, how voters cast their ballots, and how those votes are counted and verified.

To understand the importance of election integrity, imagine a house. The house, in this case, represents the democratic system of governance while the foundation, invariably under the surface, but essential in holding the structure up, represents election integrity. Without a firm foundation, the structure is in danger of crumbling.

When we look at the concept of voting rights, it encompasses a broader spectrum. Voting rights ensure that each citizen within the voting age has an equal opportunity to cast their vote without discrimination. These rights guarantee that the will of the people is reflected in their governance. In essence, voting rights are the bricks and mortar of this democratic house, allowing us to shape it according to our collective will and ideals.

However, these rights are not just about casting votes. They also encompass how votes are counted, how election information is disseminated, and how voters are protected from disenfranchisement. It is crucial to keep in mind that simply participating in the voting process is not enough; the process must be transparent, accountable, and secure.

Over time, numerous laws and reforms have been instituted to promote the principle of 'one person, one vote'. Despite these efforts, events and allegations that question the integrity of elections periodically emerge. These occurrences erode public trust and demand our attention and understanding.

Election integrity has many facets. It includes the technical aspects such as the security of voting machines and databases, and the process of tallying and verifying votes. It also focuses on the less tangible but equally important elements like voter confidence in the system, the neutrality of parties managing the election, and the prevention of misinformation that could undermine the electoral process.

A strong electoral system also demands the mitigation of corruption and manipulation. These malpractices create an environment where legitimate votes are diminished or negated, distorting the true will of the people. Notably, creating robust mechanisms to tackle these challenges are of paramount importance.

Although the focus is often placed on protecting the system from external threats, internal vulnerabilities cannot be overlooked. The protection of the voting infrastructure from internal threats is as crucial as its shield from external attacks. This is where the role of rigorous audits and checks and balances come into play.

Another critical aspect of election integrity and voting rights is access. The ability to conveniently register to vote and to have easy access to polling stations are key to meaningful electoral participation. Certain groups, particularly the economically disadvantaged and people with disabilities, may face more significant challenges in accessing polling places or obtaining required identification.

In addition, voters must have trust in the election results' veracity. Ensuring a transparency of process and a thorough verification of the results helps maintain the public's confidence in the overall electoral system. Therefore, it is vital to communicate the accuracy, security and robustness of the process to the general public.

The interplay of laws, enforcement mechanisms, institutional support, and public education are key in promoting and protecting election integrity and voting rights. In other words, they are a multifaceted problem requiring comprehensive and systemic solutions.

Political discourse and public sentiment toward election integrity and voting rights are fluid and continuously evolving. Invariably, this dynamic is driven by various factors such as societal changes, technological advancements, court rulings, and legislative changes.

Historically, the struggle for universal suffrage showcased the importance of voting rights, and to this day, these themes remain intimately connected to civil liberties. It's compelling to reflect on the evolving dimensions of election integrity and voting rights – how they form the core of democratic societies and reflect the changes within these societies.

Indeed, the exploration of election integrity and voting rights goes beyond the act of voting itself. It's a lens through which we view the health of our democracy, the balance of power, and the progression or regression of our civil liberties.

The ultimate goal is a system where every eligible voter can conveniently cast their vote, knowing that it will be accurately counted and verified, and believe in the process's fairness, irrespective of the election's outcome. This is the essence of election integrity and the sanctity of voting rights, crucial for sustaining the democratic miracle.

Republican Stance on Election Integrity / Voting Rights has long played a central part in the party's agenda, reflecting its commitment to a system that ensures every legal vote counts. The crux of this perspective revolves around measures intended to protect against fraud and uphold the integrity of the electoral process. However, the implementation and effects of these measures have fuelled intense debate, especially in today's politically polarized climate.

In the broad strokes, Republicans advocate for stricter voting laws as a way to enhance election security. They argue that tighter regulations, including voter ID requirements, are necessary to deter and detect voter fraud. Supporters posit that these safeguards ensure only eligible citizens participate in elections, thereby maintaining the credibility of the election results.

Some Republicans have voiced concerns about the expanding accessibility of mail-in ballots, particularly in light of recent changes introduced during the Covid-19 pandemic. Drawing from these apprehensions, efforts have been made by some Republican lawmakers to roll back expansions of mail-in voting, citing the potential for increased fraud risk. Simultaneously though, many of these concerns are contradicted by numerous studies showing that voting fraud in all forms is statistically very rare in the United States.

The Republican's stance also encompasses the support for periodic purging of voter rolls, claiming it eliminates inaccuracies and validates the registration systems. This includes removing entries of those voters who have moved, died, or haven't voted in recent elections. Critics, however, argue that this can lead to incidents of eligible voters being mistakenly purged from the rolls.

As Republicans stand firm on these approaches to protect electoral integrity, the consequences of these policies are often subject to contention. Critics hold that the implementation of restrictive voting laws and roll purgings can disproportionately impact certain demographics, particularly minority voters and those from lower income backgrounds. They assert that these groups are less likely to possess requisite IDs or find it harder to vote under more restrictive conditions, a criticism which Republicans typically refute by pointing towards the need for universal fairness and systemwide consistency in voting regulations.

The Republican stance on voting rights and election integrity continues to evolve and shift, particularly in our current socio-political climate. As we move forward, the challenge lies in striking a delicate balance between maintaining election integrity and ensuring that every eligible citizen can exercise their democratic right to vote.

It's essential for the informed voter to comprehend these stances and debates as they navigate the complexities of the democratic process and cast informed votes. You, as that voter, play a crucial role in understanding and engaging with these critical issues. It becomes an integral part of fostering bipartisan collaboration and moving forward, respecting the bipartisan battlefield.

Democratic Stance on Election Integrity / Voting Rights steers us towards a core pillar of democratic governance – the right to vote. Democrats believe in election integrity, but their emphasis primarily lies on making voting as accessible as possible to every eligible citizen. Their main contention is that a more extensive and inclusive electorate will lead to more democratic and representative decision-making.

Historically, Democrats have been buoyant proponents of policies aimed at expanding voter access. This includes measures like automatic voter registration, extending early voting, promoting mail-in voting, enabling same-day registration, and re-enfranchising people who have completed felony sentences. They assert that these measures drastically reduce the barriers to vote, thereby ensuring larger participation.

On the flip side, protecting election integrity is intrinsically linked with safeguarding voting rights. Democrats firmly oppose efforts that could suppress voters or disproportionately impact community groups, low-income individuals, and people of color. For instance, they resist strict voter ID laws and advocate for the restoration of the Voting Rights Act of 1965, a part of which was struck down by the Supreme Court in 2013.

While advocating for these provisions, Democrats stress the importance of making elections more secure and transparent. They push for paper ballot backups and routine post-election audits to ensure the veracity of the results. Though they resist claims of widespread voter fraud that has not been backed by substantive evidence, they do not dismiss the importance of election security.

In recent years, Democrats have pushed for comprehensive legislation to achieve these ends. The most notable among these is the 'For the People Act', which aims to bring about changes in voting access, campaign finance, and ethics in governance. Despite the critique of being too broad and overreaching, Democrats argue that such comprehensive reforms are essential to preserve the democratic nature of America's electoral process.

By focusing on voting rights, Democrats seek to affirm a core democratic principle - that every voice matters and every vote counts. Though achieving this objective is far from easy, they believe that it is essential for the integrity and reputation of American democracy.

In conclusion, the Democratic stance on election integrity and voting rights revolves largely around expanding access and removing barriers to voting, while also emphasizing the importance of secure and transparent elections. It's an approach that underscores their dedication to ensuring that every eligible citizen is able to participate in the democratic process.

Education Reform

Next in the lineup of critical political issues is education reform. An investment in knowledge pays the best interest, as Benjamin Franklin famously noted. Your understanding of education policy can ensure this interest benefits not only individual students but the nation as a whole.

Education reform is an expansive term that encompasses a multitude of areas, such as teaching quality, school funding, student safety, and curriculum standards. As a topic that directly affects the future of our society, education reform is often viewed with immense seriousness and urgency by voters and politicians alike. However, the pathways to achieving this reform can greatly differ.

In the United States, the provision of public education comes with some complex dynamics. The federal government, state governments, local governments, and school districts all have their roles in administering and financing education. Yet, despite the number of players involved, the objective remains the same: to deliver an educational experience that prepares students for success, based on a high standard of learning.

A recurring issue in education reform is educational equity. The aspiration is to ensure that every child, regardless of where they live or their socio-economic status, receives a quality education. However, how we define a 'quality education' is usually under scrutiny. While some emphasize high test scores as a measure of quality education, others argue that a holistic approach focusing on individual student growth and potential should be the gold standard.

Key among education reform discussions is the question of standardized testing. With the introduction of laws like No Child Left Behind and the Every Student Succeeds Act, standardized testing has been increasingly standardized in American schools. However, the conversation around the efficacy and fairness of these tests remains constant. Critics argue that standardized testing does not accurately reflect a student's full academic potential, considering that learners have diverse intelligences which can't be comprehensively assessed by a single standard measure.

Another controversial aspect of education reform is the school funding. It is an unarguable fact that schools need adequate funding to function effectively. Yet, in many cases, school budgets are tied to local property taxes, which has perpetuated a system where schools in wealthier districts have more resources than those in low-income areas.

The matter of how to equitably distribute school funding to ensure all students receive high-quality education is a primary concern in education reform.

The school choice movement has also received attention as part of the education reform debate. The movement is built around the idea that parents should have the freedom to choose their child's school. Such options include traditional public schools, charter schools, magnet schools, private schools or even homeschooling. However, the issue of how to maintain public oversight and accountability in these diverse educational setups is a subject of discussion and debate.

Charter schools, in particular, represent an evolving dimension of the school choice discussion. These are publicly funded independent schools that are given greater autonomy in return for greater accountability. While champions of charter schools tout them as innovative alternatives to traditional public schools, critics caution about potential lack of oversight and uneven distribution of resources.

Alongside school choice and funding discussions, the topic of academic standards and curriculum draws major attention. The question of what students should learn in schools, and how those learnings should be measured, is far from settled. Varied perspectives argue whether academic benchmarks should be set at a national, state, or local level.

Implementation of digital education and technological resources in classrooms is yet another aspect of education reform. As the world becomes increasingly digitized, there's a push to integrate technology into classrooms effectively. However, the 'digital divide' conundrum, highlighting the gap between students who have access to technology and those who do not, remains a challenge to be addressed.

The topic of school safety has emerged with urgency in the wake of school shootings, bullying, and other safety issues. While the urgency surrounding this issue is clear, devising techniques that ensure the physical and emotional safety of students, without compromising the educational environment, presents its own set of challenges.

Moreover, teacher pay and teacher quality are also cardinal points in the conversation around education reform. The critical role that teachers play in shaping future generations is undisputed, yet the profession often faces low pay and high stress, which may deter talented individuals from pursuing a teaching career. More robust teacher training and development programs, coupled with better remuneration, are often mentioned as ways to address these issues.

As appealing as the idea of optimal education reform might be, the path toward achieving it is surely not linear. It's a convoluted maze of divergent viewpoints and tangled policy proposals. As an informed voter, your understanding of the varied dimensions surrounding education reform can play a crucial role in shaping the educational landscape for future generations.

Republican Stance on Education Reform Turning the page to education reform, Republican perspectives typically emphasize greater autonomy for local control, parent choice, fiscal responsibility and accountability, preparing students for the job market, and free market competition between schools.

Integral to the Republican mantra is the belief in the power and prudence of local government. When it comes to education, they maintain that decisions about what is taught in schools as well as school management should be left as much as possible to local communities and states rather than federal intervention. They advocate for a less tangled web of bureaucratic regulations that, they contend, often hinder local innovation and implementation of effective educational practices.

Additionally, Republicans champion parent choice in education, including support for charter schools, home schooling, and voucher or tax credit programs which allow parents to send their children to private or religious schools. They argue that when parents have more options and schools have to vie for students, there is naturally a higher level of competition, promoting better overall quality.

Another cornerstone of Republican education reforms is fiscal responsibility. Republicans often express concern over what they see as excessive spending on traditional public school systems, arguing that throwing more money into the school system is not the answer to the education problem. They propose funding mechanisms that encourage schools to be more efficient and accountable for student achievement metrics.

Republicans also underscore the importance of integrating practical skills and career-readiness programs into the curriculum to help prepare students for the job market. They believe in the necessity of equipping students with real-world skills in manual work, technology, and entrepreneurship. To this end, there is also a strong Republican focus on expanding vocational and technical education to better support diverse student interests and career paths.

Throughout these policy measures, Republicans are banking on the free market to drive education improvements. They assume that when schools compete for students and funding, the quality of education will naturally rise. They perceive competition, choice and local control as catalysts for improvements in American education.

However, the effectiveness of these strategies remains a contentious issue. Critics of the Republican stance assert that relying too heavily on market principles can lead to social inequality and uneven outcomes in education. Nevertheless, all elected officials, Republican or otherwise, must grapple with the crucial task of developing an education system that effectively serves the diversity and dynamism of America's learner population.

Democratic Stance on Education Reform When it comes to the Democratic stance on education reform, make no mistake, they approach the subject with a strong emphasis on equity, accessibility, and quality. Democrats typically advocate for increased investment in public schools, universal early education, free community college, and steps to reduce the burden of student loan debt. They often argue education is an integral part of societal well-being and a key player in ensuring long-term economic success.

The Democratic view on education reform highlights the need to infuse funds into the public education system. They believe that investing in education is an investment in the country's future. Enhanced school infrastructure, increased teacher salaries, and smaller class sizes are some of the listed priorities. The fundamental idea is to ensure all students, irrespective of their socio-economic background, receive the best possible education to equip them for an increasingly competitive global economy.

Universal pre-school education is another predominant aspect of the Democrats' education platform. The belief is that early childhood education equips children with foundational knowledge, better preparing them for their academic careers. Accessible and high-quality pre-school education is seen as a vital step in leveling the academic field for children from various socio-economic backgrounds.

The Democrats' education reform strategy also encompasses higher education. They advocate for free community college education, aiming to make higher education more accessible and less burdensome for millions of Americans. This stance is based on the belief that education is a right and should be universal, unrestricted by financial barriers.

Student loan debt, a serious issue that currently affects over 40 million Americans, is also a critical aspect of the Democratic stance on education reform. Democrats typically support policies aimed at reducing, if not eliminating, the financial burden of student loans. This could range from loan forgiveness programs to caps on interest rates, with an overarching goal of making higher education more affordable and less financially stressful for students and families.

However, it's worth noting that not all within the Democratic Party hold identical views on education reform. There are disagreements over aspects such as the role of charter schools, the degree of emphasis on standardized testing, among other issues. Still, it's fair to say that Democrats generally view education as a public good that should be well-funded, accessible, high-quality, and egalitarian. It's a stance that leans towards inclusivity, with an understanding of the critical role education plays in shaping an individual's future while also serving as the backbone of our society's economic and civil landscape.

Abortion

Conversations about abortion are not new to American politics, but their significance has evolved significantly over time. The abortion debate isn't just a political issue but is deeply entrenched in moral, ethical, and religious convictions. Understanding the concept requires a detailed analysis of its historical socio-political context, varied interpretations, medical implications, and the legal framework surrounding it.

The moral and ethical questions surrounding abortion go back centuries. However, its political implications primarily began with the landmark case, Roe v. Wade, in 1973. The Supreme Court ruled that women have a constitutional right under the Fourteenth Amendment to decide to have an abortion. This decision marked a significant turning point in the role of abortion in the political, social, and legal landscapes of the United States.

Post Roe v. Wade, numerous states enacted different laws posing substantial barriers to abortion access. Arguments often center on the issue of personal autonomy and the scope of government interference in a woman's right to make decisions about her body.

Subsequent court cases have shaped the abortion discussion extensively. Planned Parenthood v. Casey (1992) reaffirmed the decision of Roe but allowed states to impose restrictions on abortion if they do not present an "undue burden" on the woman. This opened up a new door to legal, moral, and ethical debates on interpreting what constitutes an "undue burden."

The medical community's perspective on abortion is nuanced. It often entails a careful balance between protecting the health and mental well-being of the woman and considering the viability and potential rights of the fetus. As medical technology has progressed and viability outside the womb has become possible at earlier stages of pregnancy, the abortion conversation has reflected these changes.

From a societal viewpoint, the abortion discussion straddles multiple dimensions, the most significant of which is often the question of gender equality. Supporters of abortion rights argue that limiting access to safe, legal abortions can compromise a woman's autonomy, economic stability, and overall health and well-being.

Entwined intricately with the societal viewpoint is the economic perspective. Supporters often point to studies showing that reducing access to abortion can lead to an increase in poverty rates among women and a decline in their educational attainment and career advancement. Conversely, critics argue that state resources could be better used elsewhere than funding abortions.

Another view often considered is the religious perspective. Many religious denominations in the United States have established doctrine and opinions on abortion, most often citing respect for the sanctity of life from conception. However, perspectives within religious communities can be as diverse as those in the broader public.

Beneath the umbrella of abortion politics is the issue of sex education and access to contraceptives. Proponents of comprehensive sex education and increased access to contraceptives argue that such measures can effectively prevent unwanted pregnancies, consequently reducing the number of abortions.

One cannot consider the abortion question without acknowledging the role of advocacy groups. On both ends of the spectrum, groups advocate vigorously for their stance, mobilizing public opinion, lobbying policymakers, and contributing to election campaigns.

Polarization over abortion lies at the heart of American political discourse. It lives on the national stage, visible in presidential and congressional elections, Supreme Court confirmation battles, and federal and state legislation. However, opinions aren't strictly bifurcated; shades of grey exist, which can often be drowned out by the louder, more extreme voices.

The future of the abortion debate in the U.S. is tethered to ever-evolving social, legal, scientific, and political norms. The shifting composition of the Supreme Court, the fluctuating control of the legislative branch, and the influence of public opinion make the prognosis uncertain.

Whether one identifies as pro-choice or pro-life, keeps faith at the center of their stance, or views it purely from a legal, medical, or societal perspective, understanding the intricacies involved in the abortion debate becomes crucial. As political discussions continue to cement and challenge the rights and regulations surrounding abortion, equipping oneself with these insights is fundamental.

Republican Stance on Abortion is a subject filled with deep conviction and strong beliefs. Put plainly, many Republicans identify as "pro-life." This perspective is grounded in the idea that life begins at conception and that the unborn child possesses an intrinsic right to life, which should be protected above all else. It's essential, however, to remember that this belief is not a monolith within the Republican party. There are layers, exceptions, and some Republicans support different facets of pro-life legislation. For example, some may support exceptions in cases of rape or incest, while others maintain a firm "no exceptions" policy.

To provide a bit of historical context, it's worth noting that the Republican anti-abortion stance was undergirded by the landmark Supreme Court ruling *Roe v. Wade* in 1973. Challenging this judgment has been a significant rallying point for many Republicans who see the decision as an overstep of judicial power. Many Republicans favor the idea of states individually determining their abortion laws, arguing that a one-size-fits-all approach disregards the diversity of cultural, moral, and philosophical beliefs held across different regions.

Furthermore, it would be remiss not to mention that the Republican stance on abortion is often interwoven with religious beliefs. Many Republicans who are deeply rooted in conservative Christian traditions believe that life is a sacred gift from God, and thus, any action seen as intentionally disrupting this gift is immoral.

In recent years, the GOP's efforts to limit abortion access have included passing stricter laws at the state level, advocating for conservative judges in federal courts, and lobbying for restrictions on federal funding for abortion services. These tactics aim not only to limit access but also to drive legal disputes that may gradually weaken the *Roe v. Wade* precedent or ultimately see it overturned outright.

It's important to reiterate, however, that while the "pro-life" perspective is prominent among Republicans, it does not represent the views of all Republicans. There is a cohort of Republicans who are "pro-choice," believing that the decision to have an abortion ties into individual liberty and the right to privacy. While smaller in proportion, they are a reminder that political affiliations and beliefs can cross traditional party lines.

Overall, the Republican stance on abortion hinges on a powerful mix of moral principles, respect for human life, state autonomy, judicial philosophy, and the concept of individual liberty. It's a complex issue that triggers intense debate not only between Republicans and Democrats but also within the Republican party itself. As such, understanding this issue in its entirety requires one to move beyond simple labels to appreciate these nuances in perspectives.

Democratic Stance on Abortion is fundamentally rooted in the belief of safeguarding reproductive rights and personal autonomy. The Democratic Party emphasizes that decisions related to pregnancy, including the decision to have an abortion, ought to reside with the women involved and not be dictated by the state or any other external entities.

Widely recognized under the banner "pro-choice," Democrats support the landmark Supreme Court ruling of Roe v. Wade in 1973, which asserted that the constitutional right to privacy extends to a woman's liberty to choose whether to have an abortion.

The Democrats advocate for the protection of women's access to safe and legal abortion. They contest laws designed to obstruct or strategically limit this access, such as targeted restrictions on abortion providers (TRAP laws) that impose medically unnecessary requirements on clinics. Democrats also oppose "personhood" efforts that would criminalize abortions or limit access to contraceptives by giving legal rights to a fertilized egg.

Furthermore, the Democratic Party maintains that women require affordable access to reproductive healthcare, including abortion services. This is evidenced by their support for federal funding for Planned Parenthood, a significant provider of family planning and related health services. They fundamentally believe that the ability to control one's reproductive health is not only a constitutional right but also a critical factor in gender equality and economic stability. This belief extends beyond national borders; Democrats typically oppose the "global gag rule," which limits funding for international organizations that offer or inform about abortion.

Beyond the access and availability of abortion services, Democrats broadly support comprehensive sex education and contraception access in an effort to reduce the incidence of unintended pregnancies.

They consider these strategies as integral elements of effective, prevention-oriented public health policy.

The Democratic stance on abortion is hopefully clear now: to uphold the autonomy of women and ensure that they are able to make personal health decisions without undue governmental interference. However, it's key to note that within this essential alliance, perspectives may differ. Nuances aside, though, the party's core position remains the same, advocating for choice, healthcare access, and privacy.

Inflation

The increasing rise in the prices of goods and services, known as inflation, has remained a critical political issue in the United States. Generally, inflation is precipitated when demand outpaces supply, leading to higher prices and lessening the purchasing power of consumers. As prices rise, a unit of currency buys progressively less. Yet, it's important to remember that a little inflation isn't always bad; economists argue that a small amount can occasionally please the economy by stimulating spending and investment.

When examining this issue, rising inflation rates can impact the economy profoundly. For instance, as costs rise, people's purchasing power drops. This decrease can result in less consumption, impacting the economic growth negatively. If inflation becomes too high, it can lead to economic instability, with people losing confidence in the value of money.

Contrarily, a persistently low inflation rate, or deflation, can have dire economic consequences as well. Such a situation might result in an economic downturn. Many economists argue that an optimal rate of inflation sits in the 'Goldilocks zone' – not too high and not too low.

Inflation rates don't operate in a vacuum. Several factors influence these rates, including monetary policy and the supply of goods and money. In this regard, the Federal Reserve plays a significant role in managing inflation rates by manipulating interest rates, buying and selling government bonds, and adjusting the amount of money banks are required to keep in reserve.

The topic of inflation affects every individual and business in the country. It's a part of daily life, and everyone feels its impacts, whether they're aware of it or not. From the price of your morning coffee to the cost of a new car, inflation subtly, but decidedly, influences consumer behavior.

Inflation can have a broad socio-economic impact as well. When inflation rates are high, fixed-income individuals like retirees or people on social security can find their purchasing power diminished, which often leads to a lower standard of living. On the other end of the spectrum, businesses face higher costs and may have to make tough decisions, which can result in job losses or sparse hiring.

Policies related to inflation are often a contentious aspect of political discourse. Different policies can impact various sectors of the society differently, leading to disagreements about how inflation should be managed. Some parties prefer policies that emphasize price stability, while others may be inclined towards policies that prioritize employment levels over inflation rates.

When discussing inflation, it's worth noting that inflation rates can fluctuate for various reasons, making it difficult to find a one-size-fits-all solution. Factors such as a country's monetary and fiscal policies, supply of goods and services, demographic changes, and expectations about future inflation rates are all pieces of the puzzle that policymakers have to consider.

Inflation control is also a global issue. Countries are deeply interconnected, and inflation in one country can spill over into other economies. This interconnectedness means it's in every nation's interest to promote stable inflation levels worldwide. On the policy front, achieving this goal takes considerable coordination among different countries and international institutions.

The task of managing inflation is further complicated by the small margin for error. Policy decisions meant to control inflation can potentially over-correct and cause a downturn in economies. Therefore, keeping a steady guiding hand on the economy's steering wheel requires patience, and above all, experience along with the knowledge of when to intervene and when to allow the market to correct itself.

Hence, understanding inflation is integral to making informed political decisions. It's a complex beast that requires in-depth knowledge about economics and finance. The stakes are high with inflation management, with people's livelihoods and the health of the economy often hanging in the balance.

As voters, it is essential for us to delve deeper into understanding the dynamics of inflation. The upcoming sections aim to enlighten readers about the Republican and Democratic stances on inflation. As we delve deeper into these views and analyze their potential impacts on the economy and individuals, we encourage you to critically examine these positions to make an informed decision at the ballots.

It's vital to understand that any discussion about inflation doesn't take place in isolation. It's intertwined with many other issues, including employment, income inequality, the budget deficit, and more. We will highlight the interlinking threads throughout this chapter and the subsequent sections, so as to provide a comprehensive understanding of the implications of our decisions at the polling station.

Republican Stance on Inflation Turning the page toward understanding the Republican stance on inflation, one will notice that the party's basis is largely rooted in monetarist economics. Monetarists, like the highly-revered Milton Friedman, argue that inflation is, fundamentally, a result of excess money supply. Consequently, Republican representatives often prioritize strict money supply control to ensure economic stability.

Many Republicans contend that monetary expansion can cause a temporary boost in economic activity, but, in the longer-term, it may result in damaging inflationary pressures. Therefore, they suggest prudent fiscal policies, that resist the temptation of short-term monetary stimulus, to ward off potential future inflation.

Somewhat contrary to this outlook, however, is the historical proclivity of some Republican administrations to run substantial budget deficits. Such spending, these factions argue, is necessary for national defense or to stimulate economic productivity through necessary infrastructure or other investments. But they acknowledge the risk of these deficits triggering inflation, and thus they often pair them with calls for other areas of spending restraint or future fiscal consolidation.

Furthermore, Republicans have typically voiced concerns about potential distortive roles that government can play in the economy. They argue that unnecessary regulations, excessive taxation, and overprotective labor laws can result in inefficiencies that trigger price increases. Therefore, they advocate for a free market economy as a deterrent of inflation, stressing that the invisible hand will ultimately maintain economic equilibrium.

Republicans also emphasize the need for the Federal Reserve to remain independent, so it continues to prioritize maintaining low and steady inflation. They argue that central bank decisions shouldn't be influenced by political short-termism and reiterate the importance of a sound and stable monetary policy. The better such policy, they argue, the better the U.S. economy can maintain beneficial rates of inflation.

Finally, the Republican lens often views inflation as an important signal to guide economic policy. Rather than seeing it as an economic enemy, many Republicans perceive inflation as a beacon, highlighting potential misalignments in fiscal or monetary policy. If modified accordingly, these misalignments can bring back economic vibrancy and price stability.

The Republican stance on inflation, like that of any ideological group, cannot be universally generalized. Views of inflation are very much contingent on the individual's economic perspective, immediacy of perceived threats, and general political views. It's important to grasp these nuances and remember that understanding any political matter usually means navigating a spectrum of belief rather than a monolithic viewpoint.

Democratic Stance on Inflation As we've traversed the terrain of critical political issues, inflation emerges as a focal point. Addressing inflation isn't just about numbers or convoluted economic theories. For Democrats, it's about real people with real livelihoods.

From Democrat's lens, inflation isn't an isolated issue. It's wound into the larger fabric of economic policy, employment, and wage growth. The party leans heavily toward policies that stimulate economic growth while maintaining a cautious vigilance on inflation. It's a delicate balance to strike, and the Democrats' approach reflects this complexity.

The Democratic view perceives inflation as an economic symptom rather than the disease itself. It's viewed as an outcome that can be influenced by a slew of other factors. Therefore, efforts to keep inflation in check are often embedded in broader stances on wage increase, job security, and poverty reduction. For Democrats, tackling inflation isn't merely an act of policy but also a strategy of prevention through the upward mobilization of living standards for the middle class and the less fortunate.

The Democrats push explicitly for measures that boost domestic consumption and employment, such as minimum wage laws and increased government spending on social programs and infrastructure. These actions, though seemingly earmarked as spendthrift by critics, are intended to energize the economy and stimulate growth. The trick lies in ensuring these measures promote stable inflation and not a runaway price hike.

There lies an innate understanding within the Democratic party that unchecked inflation can eat away the real income of families, drive up costs, and destabilize the economy. The party acknowledges the fears of high inflation rates and consistently backs Federal Reserve's autonomy in implementing policies to maintain inflation targets – a testament to their commitment to steady economic growth.

Despite their focus on uplifting living standards and reducing income inequality, Democrats don't turn a blind eye on the potential perils of high inflation. It's a dance between stimulating growth through government spending and retaining inflation within acceptable bounds. It's about striking the right balance between helping struggling families and keeping the economy in check.

The Democratic stance on inflation showcases their commitment to economic growth, but not at the costs of causing undue economic hardship to everyday Americans. It's a balancing act of economic growth, wage increases, and inflation control designed to maximize societal wellbeing. With any policy decision that deals with the ever-volatile field of economics, the key lies in the execution and continual adaptation of strategies.

So, as we move forward in this discourse, the Democratic perspective on inflation serves as a mirror reflecting their broader understanding of and approach to economic policy. While inflation can stir up fears, it's essential to understand how each political party views this issue through their lens and how they propose to handle it.

Budget Deficit

The budget deficit is one of the critical political issues that keeps surfacing in the discourse of American politics. Let's take a personal finance metaphor to make it simpler - when your monthly expenses exceed your income, you're running a deficit. In the context of the federal government, when the expenses (such as military, infrastructure, social welfare, etc.) outweigh the revenues (principally from taxes), the government is operating under a budget deficit.

Understandably, running a deficit can seem a red flag. However, in the sphere of economics, deficits aren't always an indication of poor economic health. In fact, it is common practice for nations, including the US, to use deficit spending as a tool to stimulate economic growth. When the government spends more, it can result in increased demand for goods and services, higher business profits, and job creation, leading to economic expansion.

However, the challenge lies in carefully managing the deficit. When deficit spending is excessively high or conducted recklessly, it can lead to negative outcomes such as inflation, an increase in public debt, and eventual economic instability. The predicament is akin to using a credit card – wise use can accrue benefits, but unrestrained spending can lead to crushing debt.

Now that we've established a basic understanding of budget deficits, let's delve into the broader implications. For starters, budget deficits can directly influence interest rates. It goes like this, to finance a deficit; the government borrows money by issuing Treasury bonds. When the supply of these bonds increases, their price drops, and interest rates rise. This increase in interest rates can affect the cost of mortgages, car loans, and other personal credit, which can slow down consumer spending and inhibit economic growth.

Second, budget deficits have a way of increasing national debt. Not to be confused with the deficit, the national debt is the sum of all previous deficits, minus the amount the federal government has paid towards previous debts. While a budget deficit can act as a tool for economic stimulation, a continually growing national debt can hint at a more significant systemic issue and an unsustainable economic practice.

Moreover, budget deficits can lead to a dependency on foreign capital as the government often sells its debt to foreign investors.

Overdependence on foreign investors puts the country at a disadvantage - it diminishes its standing and provides foreign entities leverage over its policies.

Furthermore, deficits may also crowd out private investment. As the government competes with the private sector for loans and investment, an increased demand can increase interest rates, and thus the cost of borrowing for business investments. This situation could potentially reduce the overall level of economic activity.

Deficit spending, however, is not always doom and gloom. During economic downturns, such as recessions or depressions, increased government spending can counteract the decline in private sector spending. This economic booster shot is known as fiscal policy, and it played a vital role in the recovery after the Great Depression and more recently, the Great Recession.

Additionally, the deficit can finance public investments like education, healthcare, or infrastructure. These investments can foster improved productivity and quality of life, yielding long-term economic dividends. The challenge is identifying 'good' deficits, i.e., those that foster sustainable growth, versus 'bad' deficits contributing to unnecessary expenditure and burdening future generations with debt.

Also, it's crucial to keep in mind that not all entities view the budget deficit from the same lens. Credit rating agencies, for example, primarily focus on the likelihood that a government will default on its debt. A budget deficit in itself does not necessitate a higher risk of default, especially if the borrowed money spurs substantial economic growth.

As such, context is everything when we talk about budget deficits. How large are they relative to the economy? For how long have they been running? What are they being used to finance? And crucially, what is the government's plan to bring spending back in line with revenue?

Not to diminish the weight of tackling budget deficit and long-term debt, but it's important to see it as one among many factors influencing the economy. One must not lose sight of other pressing issues such as income inequality, unemployment rates, or environmental costs, all with their own significant impacts on the economic pulse of the nation. Balancing these concerns is like walking a tightrope - leaning too far in any direction can throw the entire system off balance.

There is no universal remedy or spell that can cure all. Each era demands a unique blend of fiscal restraint, strategic investment, and economic stimulation. The budget deficit, in this context, is not a prophecy of doom but a tangible representation of the nation's economic policy choices and a crucial part of the economic puzzle that needs careful handling. If managed wisely, deficits can be a valuable tool used to set the long-term economic health of the nation and ensure prosperity for generations to come.

Republican Stance on Budget Deficit has been a topic surrounded by controversy and misunderstandings, therefore it's crucial to shed light on this perspective with the aim of providing a comprehensive understanding.

The modern Republican stance on the budget deficit traditionally leans towards reducing federal spending and maintaining fiscal responsibility. Often stitching a solution through the fabric of austerity measures, their argument zeroes in on the need to curtail government spending as a pathway to achieve a balanced budget.

In order to mitigate the budget deficit, Republicans support reducing non-defense and discretionary spending. They argue for a smaller government presence, with less regulatory intervention, a stance that clearly embodies the essence of free-market capitalism. Reduction in welfare programs, social services, and subsidies comprise some of the measures that Republicans advocate.

Republicans also view tax cuts as a catalyst for economic growth. According to them, these cuts provide an incentive for businesses to invest and create jobs, which in turn can modulate tax revenues. This stream of thought is underpinned by the "supply side" economics theory also famously referred to as "trickle-down" economics.

However, it's important to note that all Republicans aren't uniform in their vista regarding the deficit. There is a spectrum of beliefs within the party, with some expressing greater concern about the deficit than others. For instance, fiscal conservative Republicans or deficit hawks emphasize the cruciality of containing the deficit, while other Republicans make room for deficit spending in certain circumstances, particularly for defense purposes or tax cuts.

And yet, critics argue that the Republican implementation of tax cuts, particularly those that are most beneficial to the wealthiest Americans, can exacerbate income inequality and potentially inflate budget deficits. They point to times in recent history when tax cuts did not stimulate the expected levels of economic growth, and deficits grew.

The stance on budget deficit is a remarkably intricate part of the Republican ideological framework and it forms a key point of delineation from their Democratic counterparts. Understanding this stance is instrumental in appreciating the Republican political perspective in solving America's fiscal issues. It is by acknowledging such difference between, and even within, parties that we citizens can navigate the turbulent waters of policy-making and contribute to constructing a more nuanced and engaged political discourse.

Democratic Stance on Budget Deficit lies on a spectrum that ranges from economists arguing for austerity measures to shift budget deficits back towards a surplus, to a rising group that embraces modern monetary theory. The former sees budget deficits as a ticking time bomb that can undermine economic stability, while the latter believes that it can be a necessary tool under right circumstances for stimulating economic growth.

In the more mainstream view, many Democrats are firm advocates for reducing the deficit, but emphasize that reduction must be accomplished in a balanced and equitable way. This often means a combination of both spending cuts and revenue increases. They argue that spending cuts should be strategic and should avoid harming vulnerable populations or undermining essential services. They also believe that revenue increases can be achieved by making the tax system more progressive, asking wealthy corporations and households to contribute a fair share.

Historically, the Democratic Party has focused heavily on social spending, resulting in significant outlays for programs such as Social Security, Medicare, and education. As such, the Democrats are often seen as the party of welfare, prepared to run a budget deficit if it is in the service of ensuring a social safety net for the country's most vulnerable populations.

However, a faction of Democrats coming from a more pragmatic school of thought, known as 'deficit hawks', is more concerned about the potential negative implications of a high deficit, voicing the need for fiscal responsibility and budgetary sustainability. They often champion measures such as Social Security reform, healthcare reform and tax increases on high earners to reduce the deficit.

In recent years, a more radical perspective has emerged within the Democratic party, driven by proponents of Modern Monetary Theory (MMT). People who adhere to MMT believe that countries such as the U.S. that have sovereignty over its own currency should not worry about budget deficits, as long as there's underutilized economic capacity (like unemployed or underemployed workers). According to them, budget deficits can play a useful role in boosting demand, and achieving public policy priorities such as full employment and socioeconomic inclusion.

Despite having these divergent perspectives within the party, Democrats largely share the view that budget deficit reduction must not come at the expense of vulnerable populations or future economic vitality. As with any political issue, the party's stance is shaped by a diversity of opinions and changing economic theories, reinforcing that there isn't a 'one size fits all' answer to economic management.

Crime

As we move forward from the previous section, let's turn our attention to an issue that's as complex as it is substantial; Crime is yet another divisive topic occupying the space in America's political battles. We cannot turn a blind eye to its impact on society, and certainly, its handling attracts impassioned scrutiny. Highest on the agenda, two predominant aspects of crime spark ignited debate: criminal behavior and its societal effects, coupled with the broader criminal justice system and its societal ramifications.

Crime is often painted with a broad brushstroke, but it's a multifaceted issue with numerous aspects. It winds its way through discussions of drug offenses, violent crime, white-collar offenses, and the societal problems that often lay the groundwork for unlawful behavior, such as poverty, lack of education, and systemic discrimination.

Many have mused about the origins of crime. Some cite statistical links to socio-economic status and educational levels, while others gravitate towards genetics and individual temperament, or nurture's interaction with nature. However, these varied contributing factors do not limit the weight that crime carries, particularly violent crime, which resonates deeply within the American psyche.

Many instances of violent crime induce a visceral reaction of fear and a collective demand for swift justice. Serial killings, mass shootings, and actions of domestic terrorism represent the extreme end of the crime spectrum. However, even with their rarity in relation to other forms of crime, their immense impact on society maintains the enduring attention of American voters and political leaders alike.

Beyond violent crime, white-collar offenses such as fraud, embezzlement, and insider trading cut into the fabric of trust that holds the business and financial sectors together. These crimes often involve larger sums of money and result in far-reaching, long-term damage, yet the perpetrators often evade the harsh punishments meted out in the case of violent crime.

Drug offenses lie somewhere in between these two ends of the spectrum. Whether it's about possession, trafficking, or the consequences associated with drug addiction, such offenses form a significant portion of American crimes. They often tie into discussions of public health and economic instability, once again demonstrating the interconnected nature of crime with wider societal issues.

The societal impact of crime is clear-cut: it leads to harm. Whether it's the direct harm to victims or the indirect harm caused by damaged communities and broken trust, crime destabilizes society. Communities wracked by crime have higher incidences of mental health issues, family breakdown, and out-of-home placements for children. The fear of crime alters individuals' behavior, making them afraid to go out after dark, forcing businesses to close early, and generally diminishing quality of life.

This throws us onto the pathway to the criminal justice system, the societal mechanism designed to address crime and its effects. This quagmire of police departments, court systems, correctional facilities, and parole boards is tasked with maintaining law and order while ensuring the rights of accused individuals are preserved.

Police departments often find themselves in the firing line of public and political opinion, having to enforce laws that are sometimes seen as controversial or racially biased. And while many police departments strive to ensure law and order with fairness and integrity, instances of excessive force or racial profiling shred public faith in these institutions.

Once individuals enter the justice system for a crime, they're often stuck in a cycle that is challenging to break free from. Serving time in prison doesn't always facilitate rehabilitation, instead potentially perpetuating criminal behavior by exposing inmates to hardened criminals and reducing post-release employment prospects.

Moreover, the disproportionate representation of Black Americans in the nation's prisons has led to accusations of systemic racism within the criminal justice system, a controversy that has catalyzed protests and demands for criminal justice reform.

The death penalty also remains an apple of discord. For some, it's seen as a just punishment for the most heinous crimes. For others, it is viewed as inhumane, expensive, and fraught with the risk of executing an innocent individual.

As we veer towards the conclusion, it's critical to understand that tackling crime is a balancing act. It's about punishing the guilty, protecting the innocent, maintaining public safety, and supporting rehabilitation. It's about acknowledging past mistakes and effectively making changes for the better. As the subsequent sections will illustrate, both Republicans and Democrats have formulated their own stances on these overarching issues. Understanding these perspectives can assist the electorate in making informed decisions and fostering constructive political discourse.

Republican Stance on Crime diverges from the Democratic point of view on several key elements. The Republican philosophy conventionally emphasizes reprehending criminal activity, maintaining law and order, and supporting victims. Let's get into some distinctive points of this party's perspective.

The cornerstone of the Republican stance is an inclination towards strict enforcement of laws, a sentiment summarized in the concept of "law and order." Republicans often champion strong punitive measures as a deterrent to crime. This 'tough on crime' approach concentrates heavily on retribution and includes support for severe penalties, including capital punishment.

Drilling down, there's an implication in the Republican stance that strict enforcement of laws, notably on drugs and gang-related activities, will deter both minor and significant crimes. This stance is rooted in the party belief that stern punishments act as imperceptive measures to criminal activity. Thus, Republicans typically endorse initiatives that intensify sentences for drug trafficking, armed robbery, violent assaults, and other severe crimes.

Republicans also tend to push for measures that provide more jurisdiction to law enforcement agencies. They often advocate for policies that protect and support law enforcement entities in their quest to enforce law and order. At times, this support may manifest as opposition to initiatives aimed at defunding the police or seeking substantial reform of police practices.

Another component of this stance is a concern with victims' rights. Republicans usually argue that the justice system should center less on rehabilitating offenders and more on advocating for justice and compensation for victims. In response, they have proposed legislation requiring victim impact statements at sentencing hearings, safeguarding victims from their attackers, and ensuring victims have a role in the parole process.

It's essential to note that this summary doesn't encompass all Republicans' beliefs on crime. Public stances on crime and justice are varied and complex, with nuances that can't fully be covered in broad party platforms. The interpretation of these platforms can also change depending upon the political climate, individuals in power, and evolving societal views.

Moving forward, conversations about 'tough on crime' policies and their efficacy, fairness, and societal impact will surely continue. Several Republicans are beginning to question long-held positions, voicing concerns about high incarceration rates and the societal costs of prioritizing punishment over prevention. Nevertheless, the general Republican stance still leans towards strict enforcement, punitive measures, and strong backing for law enforcement and victims' rights.

Democratic Stance on Crime plays a pivotal role in shaping the party's policies and platform. Crucially rooted in the intersection of social justice issues and law enforcement, Democrats approach crime from a stance of prevention, rehabilitation, and systemic change.

Democrats tend to favor policies aimed at addressing the root causes of crime over punitive measures alone. They believe that investing in education, job training, affordable housing, and mental health services can play a significant part in crime prevention. By providing opportunities for upward mobility, they seek to address socioeconomic disparities often associated with high crime rates.

Central to the Democratic stance on crime is a commitment to reforming the criminal justice system. Party leaders advocate for reducing mandatory minimum sentences, especially for non-violent drug offenders, as well as abolishing the death penalty nationwide. An emphasis on rehabilitation over incarceration is prominent, with a focus on facilitating the successful reintegration of ex-offenders into society.

The party has also called for ending cash bail systems, which they argue disproportionately penalize low-income individuals who can't afford to post bail. Instead, Democrats propose reforms that assess an individual's risk to community safety and likelihood of attending court dates.

On law enforcement, Democrats stand committed to holding officers and departments accountable when misuse of power is evident. The party has called for increased oversight, body cameras, and implicit bias training. They believe that community policing - fostering strong relationships between officers and communities they serve - is an effective play towards trust-building and effective crime prevention.

Yet, within the Democratic Party itself, views on crime and policing vary. On one end of the spectrum, progressive members call for a robust rethinking of public safety, encapsulated in the oft-heard slogan 'Defund the Police,' intended to reallocate some police funds to social services. On the other end, more moderate members caution against such dramatic shifts, emphasizing the need for police reforms without compromising public safety.

Understanding this breadth of opinions within the party is integral to comprehending the Democratic stance on crime. Recognizing this diversity of thought helps make sense of sometimes confusing messaging and policy proposals, ultimately setting the table for more informed discussions and decisions at the ballot box.

National Debt / Debt Ceiling

Stepping into the sphere of economics, let's delve into another indispensable topic that's often at the heart of political discourse: the national debt and the debt ceiling. Understanding these concepts and their implications is vital to comprehend the oft-charged conversations surrounding them in the political arena.

First, let's define these terms for clarity. The national debt is, fundamentally, the amount of money that the federal government has borrowed, over time, to finance the deficit—the difference between government spending and revenue. This debt accrues through the issuance of securities by the Treasury, including notes, bills, and bonds primarily bought by private investors, corporations, foreign nations, and more.

The debt ceiling, on the other hand, is a cap set by Congress on the amount that the U.S. Treasury can borrow. Enacted in 1917, the concept of the debt ceiling arose to facilitate budgetary control.

However, in recent times, this ceiling has evolved to become a point of rigid contention in national politics.

To the untrained eye, the relationship between these two terms would seem straightforward: a nation's debt cannot exceed the debt ceiling. However, it's essential to realize that in practice, this relationship is more complex. Over time, Congress has regularly raised the debt ceiling, enabling the country's ongoing borrowing needs caused by already enacted tax and spending laws.

Why is understanding the national debt significant? The national debt plays an intrinsic role in our national economy. On the one hand, growth in the national debt can lead to higher interest rates, reduced investment, limited financial resources for private entrepreneurs, or even a sovereign debt crisis in the most extreme scenario. However, on the flip side, deficit spending—borrowing funds to fuel greater spending—is a common economic strategy during times of recession to stimulate demand and potentially spur economic recovery.

The monster under the bed, as some would frame it, is the notion of unchecked, runaway debt growth. Implicit in this fear is the understanding that debt must be repaid and, given a big enough debt pile, the interest alone becomes a significant burden on the national coffers. It's also worth noting that high debt levels could restrict our government's ability to meet future needs or react to emergencies such as an economic downturn, health crises, or military conflicts.

At the same time, it's critical to understand that not all debt is created equal. Essentially, government debt and household debt function differently. Households often need to adjust their budgets to live within their means, but governments have more flexibility. They can adjust both the revenue (via taxation) and expenditure sides of their balance sheets, and also have an generally unlimited lifespan to spread out their debts.

Furthermore, being the issuer of a global reserve currency adds another layer of complexity. The U.S. government borrows in the currency it itself issues—U.S. dollars. This fact aids the U.S. in managing its debt obligations in a way most nations don't have access to.

On the other side of the equation, we have the debt ceiling. Why does it exist? Ostensibly, the debt ceiling is supposed to operate as a brake on spending, with Congress needing to explicitly approve any extra borrowing. However, in practice, the debt ceiling mostly adds a politically fraught step to what would otherwise be a technical loan process managed by the Treasury Department.

The debates surrounding the debt ceiling can exacerbate economic uncertainties. One key aspect to note is that raising or suspending the debt ceiling doesn't enable new spending—it allows the Treasury to pay the bills for spending already approved by Congress. A failure, or even a perceived risk of failure, to raise the debt ceiling could signal that the U.S. may not meet its debt obligations, which has far-reaching implications, from shaking investor confidence to potentially causing global economic disruptions.

Complex as it may seem, this intricate dance of national debt and debt ceiling is something that each voter needs to grapple with. Knowledge of these issues is power—the power to comprehend the ramifications of policy decisions, the power to dissect the rhetoric of political debates, and ultimately, the power to vote intelligently.

Undoubtedly, the discussions surrounding national debt and the debt ceiling are undeniably multifaceted and even highly incendiary. While opinions on how to address these issues may differ greatly, at their heart, these are crucial elements of our nation's fiscal policy, carrying weighty implications for our country's future. Understanding the depths of these economic conundrums is not just about financial literacy—it's a cornerstone of informed civic engagement.

Republican Stance on National Debt / Debt Ceiling The Republican party often positions itself as the party of fiscal responsibility, advocating for limited government spending and lower deficits. However, this viewpoint frequently competes with the realities of political governance and massive national issues that demand huge sums of money. Still, if we were to distill their stance into its core elements, it essentially advocates for controlling the national debt and maintaining a cautious approach towards raising the debt ceiling.

Historically, the Republicans have shown a tendency to highlight the risks associated with a burgeoning national debt. They express concerns that piling up significant amounts of debt could stifle economic growth and burden future generations. Consequently, this leads them to push for federal budget cuts, lean towards spending freezes, and introduce efforts to trim down entitlement programs to alleviate the debt load. Time and again, they have stood up in Congress to voice concerns over the implications of our national debt on the country's financial health and future economic stability.

The debt ceiling, on the other hand, is viewed by the party as a necessary tool, albeit treated with trepidation. This congressionally established limit on the amount of national debt that can be issued by the U.S. Treasury serves two purposes for Republicans. First, it establishes an obstacle to unchecked government spending. Secondly, it provides them with a tool of negotiation during fiscal decision-making, giving them a seat at the negotiation table when deciding the nation's budgetary priorities.

In recent history, we've seen Republicans use the debt ceiling as a bargaining chip to push for fiscal conservatism in major legislative decisions. This strategy has been evident during high-profile showdowns in Congress, such as the debt ceiling crisis in 2011 when Republicans, driven by the Tea Party Movement, demanded significant budget cuts in exchange for their votes to increase the debt limit. While such tactics are often criticized for increasing the threat of default and fostering economic uncertainty, they remain a component of the party's political playbook.

However, this fiscal conservatism does not always translate neatly into practice. Notably, under the Trump administration from 2017 to 2021, the national debt grew by nearly $8 trillion, largely due to tax cuts and increased government spending. This highlights the challenges of maintaining strict fiscal policies in a complex and constantly evolving political environment.

While the Republican party's stance on the national debt and the debt ceiling is focused on fiscal responsibility and restrained government spending, the intersection of ideology and practical politics often blurs these ideals. Nevertheless, understanding these positions provides crucial context for their legislative actions and adds to the tapestry of political negotiation and compromise that weaves American democracy together.

Democratic Stance on National Debt / Debt Ceiling After analyzing the Republicans' view on the national debt and debt ceiling, it's equally important to understand the Democrats' stance, as both parties often show vastly differing approaches on this subject. These differences, like in many political contexts, stem from contrasting economic theories and ideological principles.

Many Democrats advocate for governmental spending on initiatives such as social safety nets, healthcare, and education, among others with the goal to stimulate economic growth and ensure societal equity. This, logically, tends to increase the national debt. However, for Democrats, the focus isn't predominantly on debt reduction but more on the benefits gained from these programs. They place faith in the Keynesian economic theory that posits government spending, even with increased borrowing, can spur economic growth, ultimately benefiting the nation's general well-being and future sustainability.

Democrats have a more unfavorable view of austerity measures that are often proposed as the solution to lower the national debt. They argue that such measures can actually impede economic growth and hinder the government's ability to invest in programs shown to reduce poverty and inequality. Moreover, they propose fortifying the economy by empowering the middle class and low-wage earners, creating more consumers and driving economic development. This potentially long-term outlook can seem risky to fiscal conservatives, but Democrats argue it holds potential for a more sustained, equitable growth.

In relation to the debt ceiling, Democrats generally view it as a necessary measure that portrays the government's reliability in satisfying its financial obligations. The party has, throughout history, been more inclined to vote for an increase in the debt ceiling, and on occasion, has even proposed its elimination. This viewpoint is grounded in the concern that the consequences of not increasing the debt ceiling, such as defaulting on the nation's debts, far outweigh the benefits of using it as a device for fiscal restraint. Some Democrats posit that the uncertainty and potential turmoil it can create in the economy simply aren't worth the political leverage it occasionally grants.

Issues surrounding the national debt and debt ceiling are complex and contentious. While Democrats see government investments and maintaining national financial commitments as worthwhile despite the increase in national debt, others may see it as an unsustainable approach. It's important for voters to carefully evaluate the potential benefits and drawbacks of these policies, and to assess how they align with their own perspectives and priorities.

Foreign Policy

Our journey into the myriad layers of critical political issues leads us now to the realm of foreign policy. If we consider the country as an individual entity, then its foreign policy can be aptly understood as the behaviour it demonstrates and the relationships it builds with the rest of the world. It's a broad sphere encompassing trade, diplomacy, security, humanitarian efforts, and a host of other sub-domains that have global reach and impact.

A nation's foreign policy reflects its economic, political, cultural, and military footprint on the global stage. In the case of a superpower like the United States, its foreign policy has global implications, influencing international relations and contributing to the shape of world politics.

To dissect this complex issue, let's first comprehend the notion of diplomacy. It's a tool, a strategy used by states to manage their relations with each other. It is diplomacy that we often witness in direct negotiations, ambassadorial engagements, and even in repelling conflicts.

Trade policies, another essential component of foreign policy, have a direct impact on a country's economy. They determine the flow of goods, services, and investments across borders. Superpowers like the United States leverage their trade policy to stimulate economic growth, protect domestic industries, or, at times, punish perceived unfair trade practices by other nations.

Often tethered to economic and trade considerations is the realm of international security. In securing national interests, nations often face threats ranging from terrorism to nuclear proliferation. The nuances of military involvement, alliances, and defense budgets become critical elements of a nation's foreign policy.

Foreign aid and humanitarian efforts form another pillar of foreign policy. Nations allocate funds and resources to support countries grappling with emergencies or development challenges. Foreign aid can be a potent tool to foster good relations, promote shared values or, quite critically, to push a strategic agenda.

Foreign policy also considers international law. Countries utilize treaties, international agreements, and organizations to manage collective action problems like climate change, human rights abuses, or nuclear proliferation. Adherence to the ideals promoted by these important legal frameworks can significantly bolster a nation's global reputation and influence.

The United States, for instance, has historically showcased a commitment to advancing democratic values worldwide. Whether it's advocating for human rights, freedom of expression, or electoral democracy, these principles often find a prominent place in American foreign policy. These initiatives have often positioned the U.S. as a global leader in upholding democratic values.

Then there's the geopolitics of energy which wields a tremendous influence on foreign policy. Access to energy resources, such as oil and gas, can direct foreign policies, shape alliances, and even spark conflicts. Energy policies have always been a considerable aspect of foreign relations and will continue to be so, especially as the world grapples with climate change and the transition to renewable energy.

Climate change, in and of itself, is another significant facet of foreign policy in today's world. It is an international issue that requires a collective global response. The policies and commitments of nations to combat climate change actively shape their international standing.

Lastly, let's not forget cultural exchange and international relations. These programs often serve as soft power tools, improving international relations, promoting mutual understanding and connecting people through arts, sports, and education.

While navigating through these complex layers of foreign policy, one thing we must always keep in mind is that foreign policy is rarely black and white. It is complex and multifaceted, often intertwining various aspects such as economics, security, humanitarian issues, and global commitments. As such, the decisions a country makes on foreign policy grounds can have far-reaching implications, not just for their nation but for the entire globe.

In conclusion, understanding foreign policy is an important part of grasping a nation's political perspective. It gives context to the nation's actions on the global stage and offers insights into its international relations strategy. Much like the other Critical political issues we've covered, foreign policy can't be distilled into a single narrative but is, instead, a comprehensive tapestry of interconnected forces and factors.

Republican Stance on Foreign Policy is largely characterized by a belief in American exceptionalism, a preference for unilateral action, a commitment to a strong military, and an emphasis on protecting American interests abroad. Republican foreign policy often advocates for robust military spending to bolster national defense and maintain America's global standing. This approach has been consistently exhibited throughout various Republican administrations, though the strategies for implementing these principles can differ based on the individual stance of the president.

One hallmark of the Republican approach to foreign policy is the concept of 'peace through strength.' This embodies the belief that a powerful military deters potential adversaries and ensures security and peace. Therefore, Republicans often favor increasing military spending, modernizing the armed forces, and maintaining a strong nuclear deterrent.

Moreover, Republicans urge for a proactive rather than reactive foreign policy. This means addressing potential threats before they pose a significant risk to American interests, even if such actions require unilateral steps. Notably, the administration of George W. Bush exemplified this in its 'preemptive strike' doctrine on Iraq.

However, the party's stance has taken a more isolationist tone in recent years, highlighted by the phrase 'America First', popularized during Donald Trump's presidency. This shift is characterized by increased skepticism towards international agreements and institutions, in favor of a focus on domestic issues and national sovereignty. This was illustrated by the withdrawal from the Paris Climate Agreement and the Iran Nuclear Deal during Trump's tenure.

Overall, the Republican Party also underscores the critical importance of promoting democratic values, human rights, and free markets worldwide. This has led to the support of sanctions against authoritarian regimes and the provision of aid to emerging democracies. Recent administrations have also emphasized the role of economic tools, like trade agreements and economic sanctions, in pursuit of foreign policy goals.

In a nutshell, while the core principles of the Republican foreign policy remain unchanged, its application has been fluid, reflecting the shifts in global dynamics and domestic politics. It's vital to remember that while the party's stance provides a broad framework, individual politicians and administrations implement these principles in their own way. The essence of Republican foreign policy, however, has always been to assert and protect American influence and interests on the global stage, using both military power and diplomatic negotiations.

Democratic Stance on Foreign Policy conjures an image of a party that pushes for global cooperation and diplomacy. The Democrats have a long-held tradition of embodying a multilateral approach, emphasizing the importance of international alliances and agreements. They acknowledge that the United States doesn't live in isolation, and its actions on the global stage have ripple effects. Hence, creating a world order that reflects shared values of democracy, human rights, and economic equity is a paramount task for Democrats when it comes to foreign policy.

Key themes of the Democratic foreign policy include strengthening alliances, promoting democracy, human rights, and strengthening institutions of global governance. It is largely an approach of international cooperation, where negotiation and multilateral dialogues are seen as cornerstones to tackle global issues. That's not to imply that Democrats shy away from taking bold decisions. There's also a strong resolve to hold nations accountable for actions that undermine peace, stability, or violate human rights.

One area of foreign policy where Democrats have shown notable commitment is in addressing global climate change. They favor recommitting the United States to international agreements like the Paris Climate Accord. They acknowledge that climate change is a global issue that requires global solutions, and the U.S. has a role to play in that.

Nuclear nonproliferation is another policy area where Democrats take a firm position. They support arms control treaties and have traditionally advocated for the continuation of agreements like the New START Treaty, a nuclear arms reduction treaty with Russia. By contrast, criticism of international organizations and agreements is less common, with Democrats generally advocating for judicious engagement with these entities.

The ethos of the Democratic foreign policy leans towards the belief that cooperation, diplomacy, and international engagement are crucial tools in the toolbox of American power. That in no way neglects the need for military strength, but rather signifies that military power is most effective when used judiciously and complemented by diplomatic and humanitarian efforts.

However, this does not mean Democrats are unified on every foreign policy issue. Like any large political group, there are varying viewpoints within the party. Differences in opinion can arise over the use of military intervention, balancing American interests versus human rights concerns, and the nature of relations with nations such as China and Russia. Yet despite these nuanced differences, the Democratic party's preference for multilateralism and diplomacy tend to take center stage.

At the end of the day, the Democratic stance on foreign policy can be summarized as a belief in the power of collective action and international diplomacy, tempered always by a commitment to

American security and values. As the world becomes increasingly interconnected, the Democratic party prioritizes using international cooperation and diplomatic channels to achieve foreign policy objectives.

Chapter 3:
Ways to Foster Bipartisan Collaboration

As we clear the fog of partisanship, we come across a path less taken yet of supreme importance: bipartisan collaboration. This often-elusive entity holds the potential to not only mend the tearing socio-political fabric, but also effectively address and resolve critical issues, delved into in the previous section, that our nation contends with. The power dynamics of party politics can be balanced through the implementation of cooperative models where decision-making comes not from strict party lines, but from a shared understanding of what is truly beneficial to the country. Emphasizing collaboration involves fostering an environment of acceptance and understanding, where intellect trumps ideology and cooperation quells corruption. This also requires shifting focus from adversarial tit-for-tat tactics to cooperative strategies. Mutual respect, focusing on common ground, and promoting dialogue over debate can ensure a productive political discourse. As we journey further into this pivotal chapter, be ready to delve into the nitty-gritty of fostering compromise and enhancing effective communication across party lines. This shift may not be easy, yet it's crucial to our nation's progress. Ultimately, the pursuit of bipartisan collaboration is less about winning, and more about weaving together the values and perspectives that truly represent the rich diversity of our nation into a coherent, effective political action.

The Need for Compromise

In the journey to creating harmony among political parties, one word comes to mind - compromise. As simplistic as the term may sound, it is a crucial determinant in ensuring bipartisan collaboration. When politicians put aside their personal and party preferences and reach a consensus for the greater good, they present an image of unity that encourages cooperation and progressive governance.

Similarly, in the public sphere, the need for compromise cannot be overemphasized. Citizens stand to benefit most when there's agreement on policies that impact their day-to-day lives. To this end, fostering an atmosphere that encourages healthy debate, respects opposing viewpoints, and promotes negotiation is key.

What we need to acknowledge is that compromise does not imply defeat. Instead, it's simply understanding that having everything one's way isn't always beneficial or feasible. In the political realm, it's recognizing that the nation's best interests supersede party priorities.

Compromise is the means by which we find common ground. It's the space between the "either-or" where productive dialogue can flourish. In politics, this often means developing hybrid policies that incorporate elements from both party platforms to meet the nation's diverse needs.

Of course, bringing the concept of compromise to life can be tough, given the entrenched party loyalties and oftentimes polarized views. However, change often starts with individuals. As such, one way to embrace compromise is by cultivating a willingness to listen and learn from those with differing viewpoints.

In the face of this polarization, it's crucial to remember that democracies thrive on diversity of thought. The existence of opposing perspectives is not a disadvantage, but the foundation that enriches our democratic fabric. Compromise enables us to harness this diversity, driving policies that work for all and not just the few.

Look at America's historical milestones, for instance. Major advances have often come about through shared recognition of a problem. From the civil rights movement to healthcare reform, none of these would have been possible without some form of compromise between stakeholders.

However, compromise is not about sacrificing principles. It's about finding a middle ground - a place where differing groups can meet, negotiate, and fashion solutions that work for everyone without betraying core beliefs.

For America to maximize her potential, it is indispensable to engage in this dance of give-and-take. Compromise encourages cooperation, builds trust, and opens doors towards finding solutions that reflect our collective interests.

Positive progress is achieved when we manage to find shared goals, even amidst differing paths. By working towards common objectives, commitment to compromise can be stressed above the more divisive aspects of party politics.

While acknowledging the difficulties of compromise, we also need to highlight its benefits. The act of compromising helps in diffusing potential conflicts, fostering understanding, and building friendships across party lines—a testament to the unity in diversity that America holds dear.

In the end, the role of compromise in fostering bipartisan collaboration is about ensuring that a vibrant democracy thrives, characterized by respect, tolerance, and the pursuit of commonly agreed objectives. As such, the need for compromise is not just a nice concept—it's an essential element in sustaining America's democratic ideals.

While we navigate through the various chapters of America's political future, let's remember that compromise is less about surrendering and more about understanding and embracing each other's perspectives. An open mind that is willing to compromise is a testament to the strength of a nation. A testament to our unity amidst our diversity.

Compromise goes beyond winning or losing—it's the enabler of progress and a tool for promoting mutual respect and understanding across the political spectrum. By embracing compromise, we give ourselves the chance to move from rigid viewpoints to an environment of constructive collaboration, uniting us all in the quest for a better America.

Effective Communication Across Parties

Breaking down the barriers that divvy up partisan lines requires a thoughtful, intensional approach. This notion chiefly applies to effective communication across parties. It works like a skill that should be consciously developed and refined; in essence, it is bridging the gap between differing viewpoints with language.

Effective communication begins with mutual respect for differing opinions. It not only recognizes someone's right to an opposing viewpoint but appreciates the diversity of thought brought into the conversation. Instituting this initial baseline of respect forms a productive foundation that is both respectful and emphatic, allowing for an open exchange of ideas.

Next, there is the aspect of active listening. Often, political conversations devolve into a clash of monologs, where each party is seeking to score points rather than understand the other's perspective. The ability to listen, to take a pause and genuinely comprehend the other person's stance, is vital in crossing the electorate divide. Keep in mind the old saying: we have two ears and one mouth for a reason.

When it comes to expressing your views, it's crucial to keep emotions in check. Passionate political discussions can quickly become heated, derailing constructive conversations. Diplomacy is the key. Practice delivering your opinion on a sensitive topic in a calm, respectful manner, without letting your emotions take charge.

Constructive and respectful conflict is another cornerstone of effective bipartisan dialogue. Accept that conflating, sometimes irreconcilable, views will emerge. However, transformation is feasible when these confrontations are processed beneficially to explore innovative ideas and solutions. Respectful disagreement leaves room for common ground.

Framing is a crucial aspect. Framing involves presenting an issue in a way that can be understood and accepted by your listener. This doesn't mean watering down your argument but can encompass adapting your language or finding common values that align with the matter at hand.

Another pivotal challenge in bipartisan communication is tackling confirmation bias, the human tendency to interpret new information as confirmation of one's current beliefs or theories. While strenuous, it's necessary. Being aware of this bias, it can become easier to catch yourself in the act of discarding or overlooking information that challenges your existing narrative.

Language, without doubt, plays a significant role in bridging political divides. Avoid snarky remarks or using demeaning language when discussing opposing viewpoints. Use polite, neutral language to participate in an open discourse that encourages understanding rather than exacerbating divisions.

Also, be patient. Changing attitudes or beliefs deeply ingrained in someone's identity cannot happen overnight. In such an instance, the aim should be to initiate a dialogue and provide a new viewpoint rather than changing someone's mind entirely.

Open-mindedness must be maintained at all times. Remember that your perspective is one of many, and others can offer valuable insights from their vantage point. This open-mindedness invites an attitude of learning rather than winning, nurturing a fertile land for productive discussions that surpass party lines.

Importantly, don't forget about follow-ups and feedback. Communication doesn't end when the dialogue ends. Maintain a continuous dialogue, show appreciation for shared new perspectives, and express openness to future interactions. This approach helps build relationships that prize understanding over division.

Remember that communication is a two-way street. Just as you expect others to respect your views, you must extend the same courtesy. Foster an environment where everyone feels heard, understood, and respected regardless of their political affiliations.

For Massive progress to be made, we have to identify what hinders effective communication in the first place. Misinformation, stereotypes, and prejudice can all undermine bipartisan dialogues. Tackling these roadblocks and creating a climate of informed, unbiased communication is the goal.

Finally, leverage the power of empathy. Raise this at the fore of your communication efforts to show that, despite belonging to different political parties, we are all a piece of a larger puzzle called society. In the end, it's not about horning in on each other's turf but about finding ways to work together for the common good.

Bipartisan collaboration is not an unattainable ideal. It just requires a willingness to understand other perspectives, an open mind, effective communication skills, and commitment. Equipped with these tools, partisan divides can be bridged more readily, culminating in progress towards a greater understanding and respect for the plurality of our political system.

Conclusion

In summary, the power to shape the future of our nation rests in the hands of the voter. Engaging in the political process demands more than merely checking a box on a ballot; it requires diligent research, a clear understanding of each party's stance on pivotal issues, and a recognition of the biases that infiltrate our political policies. It's our right, and, more importantly, our responsibility, to stack our decision making on the pillars of unbiased information, fostering a climate where ignorance loses its grip on our political sphere. Acknowledging this, we comprehend the value of compromise and effective communication amidst our fiercely bipartite battlefield. As we step into the voting booth, we carry with us the hope for a better tomorrow—a world where critical political issues are navigated with prudence and integrity. Therefore, it's crucial that we continue to evolve in our political understanding, encouraging a culture of knowledge, respect, and resilience as we navigate the complexities of our bipartisan landscape.

The Role of The Informed Voter

Having set the stage in previous chapters, let's shift our attention to the key player in the democratic arena: the informed voter. This critical figure holds a certain power in the political landscape. They possess an understanding that moves beyond popularity contests and shallow appearances. The informed voter is a driving force in the democratic process, carrying the weight of well-rounded knowledge and mindful decision-making.

Now, this raises the question, why is an informed voter so crucial to our democracy? Simply put, an informed choice is a sound choice. It involves understanding the various political perspectives, recognizing the implications of policy decisions, and being privy to current and longer-term issues. This enables the voter to make an election decision based on careful consideration rather than on superficial factors or unfounded hearsay.

Frequently, folks exhibit a tendency to vote according to party lines, whether out of allegiance, habit, or an assumed alignment of ideals. Such a trend remains even when party stances evolve or diverge significantly from the voter's interests. Here is where the informed voter distinguishes themselves. Not tied down by blind loyalty, they value knowledge and engage in an ongoing learning process.

Armed with understanding, informed voters question, reflect, and evaluate before exercising their right to vote. They research alternatives, engage in discussions, delve into the origins and consequences of policies, and seek unbiased sources of information. Consummate learners, they realize that the world is not painted in black and white, and the political landscape is far from being an exception.

Informed voting takes us a step away from polarizing rhetoric and combative politics. It fosters a more nuanced understanding of bipartisan politics, and recognizes that issues are multifaceted, with numerous possible solutions that can traverse party lines. This recognition encourages cross-party discussion, negotiation, and compromise - the foundations of effective governance.

Moreover, informed voters are less likely to fall prey to manipulation or deceit. Clear, sound facts can stand up against the incendiary sound bites that frequently cloud election campaigns. When voters are accurately informed, there is less room for misleading narratives or divisive tactics to distort the realities of political issues or candidate platforms.

The role of the informed voter extends beyond our local communities or national borders. When citizens make informed decisions, they contribute positively to preservation of democracy and political stability internationally. In our interconnected world, the choices we make domestically can resonate globally.

Being an informed voter requires effort. It's not a role acquired overnight but cultivated over time. This process calls for the curiosity to learn, the patience to understand, and the openness to change. It's a task that dares us not to remain indifferent or complacent.

Educators, media outlets, nonprofits and public figureheads have a crucial role in nurturing informed voting. They're responsible for presenting clear, objective, and comprehensive information to the public. Their role is to facilitate dialogue, encourage critical thinking, and disseminate accessible yet detailed facts about political stands, policy outcomes, and election processes.

But the ultimate responsibility rests upon us, the people. In our hands, we have the power and duty to keep ourselves informed – to ensure every vote cast is a declaration of our informed conviction, not merely the product of fleeting whims or constructed fears. We hold the strength to shape our government, and by extension, the trajectory of our nation.

Grasping the vast importance of the role the informed voter plays in our democracy, we can appreciate the impact of what may seem like a singular decision. The domino effect our votes have on public policies, national mood, and global perceptions underscores the weight and significance of this role.

As informed voters, we contain the possibility of change in our hands every election cycle. Each vote we cast can be a cog in the machine that propels our society toward a more understanding, tolerant, and just future. This fact alone illustrates the enormous power a well-informed voter wields. To quote Louis D. Brandeis, "The most important office, and the one which all of us can and should fill, is that of private citizen."

The role of the informed voter is daunting yet inspiring. It never diminishes, nor does it fade away. Instead, it waits patiently for us to realize its importance and step up. Informed voting is, at its core, a declaration of our power, an exercise in authority, and a testament to our collective potential to build the world we seek to live in.

Moving Forward: Respecting the Bipartisan Battlefield

As we carry our newfound understanding of the bipartisan landscape into the future, we need a mature perspective. We approach politics not as a winner-takes-all battle, but as a cooperative endeavor. We must remember that all discourse, no matter how contentious, stems from a shared desire to improve our nation's well-being.

First and foremost, it's essential to respect the values that emerge from the heat of the bipartisan battlefield. Everyone, regardless of political leaning, is guided by their unique experiences and perceptions, which shape their beliefs. Whether you align towards conservatism, liberalism, or find yourself somewhere in between, holding a belief is a reflection of one's lived experiences. Our stances, therefore, deserve respect.

Then we have the ballet of compromise. Compromise isn't just about giving up what we want in favor of the other party; it's about seeking a middle ground. It revolves around values, policies, and plans, with the aim of creating an arrangement in which all parties involved find a measure of satisfaction. It's crucial for us, as voters, to support politicians willing to navigate the delicate course of compromise for a prosperous future.

An understanding of the specific issues at hand is fundamental to this process. When armed with a clear comprehension of topics like healthcare reform, climate change, immigration policy, and others, voters can see beyond mere party lines. They can look at policies independently and gauge their efficacy, aiding in their choice of representatives and policy preference.

A significant hurdle in reaching this enlightened state of voting, however, is misinformation. Rumors and falsehoods have run rampant, especially with the advent of social media platforms. As voters, keeping ourselves informed about the world, politics, and the issues that matter is not just a civic duty but a necessity. Always cross-check and confirm news before accepting it as the truth.

When casting our votes, we're not just electing a person or party to power; we set the course for our nation. An understanding of each candidate and party's stance on critical issues helps us make an informed decision for the country's future.

Politics is, after all, the organizational method for defining priority areas, setting goals, and determining resource distribution. When voters understand their role in this process and are willing to embrace a bipartisan approach, the chances of attaining national progression increase exponentially.

Keeping our focus on individual policies instead of the party presenting them can also lead to a more balanced view of politics. It is no secret that party positions often polarize voters. Evaluating policies based on merit, instead of getting tangled in party biases, enables us to vote wisely.

Lastly, let's remember that the bipartisan battlefield is not a divide but a bridge. A bridge that, if crossed with understanding and a willingness for cooperation, can bring holistic growth for our nation. The respect we show to differential viewpoints will help keep our democracy thriving and open to evolution.

In conclusion, politics need not be a war. It should be a dialogue, a discussion, an exchange of ideas and beliefs in the pursuit of a shared goal - a prosperous, equitable, sustainable future.

As voters, we are the essential wheels that move the vehicle of democracy. Let's move forward, taking strides on the bipartisan battlefield with composure, understanding, and respect. Never losing sight of the shared objective - a better future for all of us.

To move ahead respectably on the bipartisan battlefield, understanding, respect, compromise, and embracing a holistic approach are manifestly integral. Just as a coin has two sides, our political system thrives on the balance provided by the two main parties. Let's carry forth this balance, accept differences, and strategize for a progressive future. Because at the end of the day, the battlefield is not a place for destruction, but rather, a place where a better, unified future is forged.

Carrying the torch of democracy forward, we can chart the best course for our nation's future. With a respect for the bipartisan battlefield, and an informed mindset, we can transform the field of politics from adversarial combat into a cooperative venture – all for a collective good.

So let's move forward, realizing the importance of individual and collective action in the political sphere, ready to respect and navigate the challenging but rewarding terrain of the bipartisan battlefield.

www.ingramcontent.com/pod-product-compliance
Lightning Source LLC
Chambersburg PA
CBHW030404290526
45785CB00004B/1904